Stock Trading for Begin

The Complete Guide to Trading and Investing in the Stock Market

Table of Contents

Introduction

Congratulations on downloading *Stock Trading for Beginners* and thank you for doing so.

The following chapters will discuss the steps you need to know to get started on the stock market. Many people worry that investing in the stock market is not for them. They may have heard stories about how some people lost their savings by jumping into a stock and risking it all. The tips and strategies in this guidebook are going to prevent you from ending up being an investor like that. Instead, this guidebook will show you how to exactly make money trading on the stock market.

Inside this guidebook, we are going to discuss everything you need to know to get started on investing in the stock market. We will start out with some basics about the stock market before moving on to how to tell the differences between some securities, how to choose a good stock, how to look over an SEC report, and even how to get the right trading platform for you to be successful.

We are also going to discuss some strategies that you can use to buy and sell the right stocks at the right time. We will look at some methods to figure the true value of a stock, as well as how to do a fundamental analysis and recognize some stock patterns. Moreover, we will discuss other strategies to make you successful. We will end this guidebook with a discussion on the best tips you can follow to help avoid a loss and gain a profit on the stock market.

There are plenty of books on this subject on the market, thanks again for choosing this one! Every effort was made to ensure it is full of useful information. Please enjoy!

Chapter 1: How to Enter the Stock Market

The stock market is a very exciting field to invest in. This is a very large industry where billions of dollars are traded each day.

There are thousands of different stocks that you can choose to trade. With its diversity, you can find a stock that interests you and works for your budget as long as you take some time to explore it. Anyone who has a little money can get into the stock market and earn an income.

While anyone can get into the stock market, it is important to be able to spend some time exploring and fully understanding it before jumping in. Those who have studied the market for some time are the ones who tend to do the best when it comes to investing.

What Is the Stock Market?

The stock market is going to refer to all parties involved in the selling and buying of shares, bonds, and other securities of a publicly listed company. An important part of the free economy, the stock markets have two segments, namely, the primary and the secondary markets.

The primary market is made up of early-stage companies, or those who are trying to sell shares in order to gain resources for themselves. They do this through an initial public offering or an IPO. Thanks to how the stock market works, companies are able to acquire funds by selling their stock to public investors. In return, these investors gain partial ownership of the company.

For the most part, long-term trends show that the market as a whole is on an upward trajectory, and many investors are interested in adding stocks to their portfolio. Many people have made their fortunes with the stock market, but you really have to study it, be disciplined, and have some sound thinking behind any investment decision.

Making money from the stock market does not have to be difficult. Just like any other kind of investment, it is possible to master and be good at this with time, practice, and lots of studying. You can easily make a living on the stock market, but you need to be rational and think through things because many people have also lost all their resources from just one bad investment. This is where the stock market gets its bad reputation.

Many investors who jump in without thinking find themselves greatly disappointed because they lost everything. If only they had started with a good strategy and invested only on what they could afford to lose, the stock market could have been their key to great success.

What Is the Difference Between Investing and Speculating?

To keep it simple, an investor is someone who decides that it is time to make their money work for them. They may use some of their own savings to purchase a stock and then earn any paid profits as long as they hold on to that stock.

Investing is going to have rules. Anyone can become an investor, but you can only get ahead in the market if you learn the right strategy and agree to stick with the rules.

When you do not act within the rules, you may become a speculator without even knowing. A speculator is someone who only pays attention to short gains. They will rush into a position and make themselves more vulnerable at the same time. Now, there is a difference between a speculator and a day trader. Day traders study the market, and they plan to be in it for a long time. They just make a lot of trades throughout the day, but they have a plan and they know what they are doing along the way.

A speculator is just someone who wants to jump in, make money overnight, and be done with it. This happened a lot with the rise of Bitcoin. Bitcoin started at $1 per coin in 2009. It steadily rose until it almost reached $20,000 a coin by December 2017. Many people jumped on to this, hoping to see another price increase and not looking at what this cryptocurrency is about. Almost overnight in early January 2018, the Bitcoin crashed down to $10,000. It now holds steady around $6,000 to $6,500 in worth.

An investor would have seen this as trouble. They would have known that they would lose money because the cryptocurrency would not stay at that level with the way it was set up. Savvy investors would have stayed away and picked another option. A speculator, however, would have joined the Bitcoin market in December and lose all their money by January.

Do not be a speculator when you join the stock market. There are times when a stock will surprise you. This may allow you to make a lot of money, but you need to concentrate on how the market works and whether it is actually a smart investment for you.

Understanding More About the Stock Market

The stock market plays a big role in driving the economy. It is characterized by trading equities and some other securities from a publicly listed company. One popular investing style in the stock market is adding funds to a public company in order to gain partor full ownership. This means the investor is entitled to some of the profits from that company. A successful investor will receive more in dividends than the capital they originally gave out.

As we mentioned, there are two types of markets, which are the primary and secondary markets.

Primary market. This is where company shares are traded through an IPO. You can also view this as a direct trade between the investor and the company.

Secondary market. This is when investors trade among themselves, while the associated company for the security is excluded.

The two factors that help determine the price of a public company's stock are the volume of shares and the value of the company. In an IPO, the company needs to stash away any windfall. Once the stock grows enough in time to generate revenue, it will be the turn of the investor to profit from it. The company, on the other hand, will not profit.

The trading of stocks occurs in an exchange. These exchanges play a role in facilitating trades between the buyers and the sellers. Most of the time, these are going to be done electronically. These exchanges are found in almost all capital cities in the world. In the United States, the two most known exchanges are the NASDAQ and the New York Stock Exchange. The U.S. Securities and Exchange Commission, or the SEC, is an independent agency of the federal government that oversees these exchanges and ensures fair play and investor protection.

Supply and demand drives the price of a stock. If there is a ton of buzz around a company, then, more investors will be interested in trading the shares of the company. Profitable companies can also see the same rise in their stock prices.

There are different types of shares that you can purchase, including, but not limited to the following:

- Ordinary shares
- B-ordinary shares
- Exchange traded funds
- Preference shares
- N-ordinary shares

There are also two types of securities that can be traded on the stock market, namely, listed and over-the-counter securities. The listed securities need to meet all the listing requirements of an exchange and must secure approval from the SEC. On the other hand, over-the-counter securities will be traded between peers and will be handled by dealers. These over-the-counter securities often do not appear on an exchange, which means they do not have to meet SEC requirements. There are times when they can prove to be a good investment, but they also involve more risk than normal securities.

Each type of stock you choose to work with will come with its own risk. You have to determine which method is going to be the best for your needs. You can choose a long-term investment in a company that is already doing well and is returning good dividends. Or, you can take a bit more risk and go with a new company that you predict will do so much better and give you huge returns in the future. As an investor, you have to know the difference between these two options. You must also have a system in place to determine how much risk you are willing to take on.

Should I Go with Stocks or Options?

Stock trading and options are the best choices when it comes to investing. Many brokerage firms will offer both these services to their investors, but how do you know which one is the best for you?

First, let us take a look at a stock. A stock is simply a fraction of ownership in a company that you can purchase. You can technically own as many shares of the company's stock as you can afford, as long as someone is willing to sell them to you.

An option is a little bit different. This is not really a form of ownership, but it is more of a right to own or trade a certain investment. You own the investment, but not a part of the company it belongs to. When you work with an option, you have the right to buy or sell a stock at a certain value within a specific period of time.

There are also no rules on how long you need to hold onto a stock. You can set a timeline on how you plan to make money, as well as the strategy that you want to go with. However, when you have an option, it will have an expiration date. This means you have until that expiration date to decide if you are going to use that option, or purchase that option. This gives you a specific time period to execute a purchase or a sale at a certain value. You can keep the option of running for as long as you would like. Some of these options last for an hour, while others even last for a few years. It all depends on which option you go with.

Stocks are a bit different. You can technically hold onto them until you die. But there are some who have a shorter timeline on holding these stocks. For example, a day trader may trade their stocks multiple times throughout the day. These investors are looking to capitalize on the little increases that occur in a stock on a daily basis. Then, there are long-term investments in the stock market where a trader will hold onto the stock for a long time, earning dividends on it each quarter.

The one you want to go with is going to depend on your level of experience in investing and how much risk you want to take on. Often, options are seen as riskier because you are betting on the price staying or moving to a specific level over time. This is the opposite for many stocks, which can stay pretty secure and can be done over the long term. Regardless of their differences, both can be great ways to earn an income and get your money to work for you!

Chapter 2: The Differences Between Stocks, Mutual Funds, Index Funds, and ETFs

When you enter into the stock market, you have several options to help you make a profit. Some people choose to work on their own and would just like to purchase individual stocks that suit their needs. Others may want to play it safe or increase their buying power by working with a mutual fund. And still, others find their trading strategy to be a bit different from either of these. Let us take a look at the differences between some of the investment choices you can make when you enter the stock market.

What Are Stocks

First, we need to look at stocks and what they are about. To keep things simple, a stock is a share in the ownership of a company. The investor who holds onto the stock has a claim on the assets and earnings of that company. The more stocks in a company you acquire, the more ownership you have in that company.

Now, this does not mean that you technically own the corporation. Owning the stock does give you some power though. When you own a stock, It means you might have the right to vote on important decisions for the company. You can also receive dividends off the profits of a company. It also allows you to sell those shares of the company whenever you want to do so.

If you are able to own the majority of the shares in a company, you will see that your voting power increases, allowing you to indirectly control the way the company goes.

As a majority owner, you may have more power to nominate and appoint the board of directors. In a publicly listed company, a shareholder gets to vote on who sits on the board. The number of your votes, however, is dependent on how many shares of the company you own.

This is important because the board directs the goals and activities of the company. The board is also involved in the appointment of people to top management roles like the chief executive officer, chief operating officer, and the chief financial officer.

Your voting power also becomes very apparent any time a company buys another. The acquiring company does not go around and buy the building, the employees, and the chairs. Instead, it goes and buys up all the shares. The company usually needs the approval of its shareholders for any proposed merger or acquisition to push through.

When you are investing in the stock market, being unable to manage the whole company is probably not that big of a deal. Most shareholders are interested in receiving dividends off the profits of the company. The more shares you own, in this sense, the larger portion of the profit you will get. There are times, however, when the company will not pay out dividends. Instead, the company will reinvest its profits back for its own growth. These are known as retained earnings, but it can still be a way to make money.

A company will issue stocks to raise capital, grow its business, and undertake new projects. There are some big differences between an investor directly buying shares from the issuing company, or from an investor buying the shares from another shareholder. When a corporation issues its stocks, they are doing it to gain money to help their growth.

When you think about investing in the stock market, the first thing you probably think about is stocks. The day-to-day price fluctuations of these stocks can be varied, but if you stick with them for the long term, they usually tend to trend upwards. If you get a bad stock, you can end up losing money as it fails. But generally, the market and the value of the stocks will continue to grow. The company gets the funding they need to expand and grow, and you get a chance to earn a profit on the dividends if you invest wisely.

Mutual Funds

Another option you can go with is mutual funds. Mutual funds are perfect for any investor who wants to be able to reduce their risks rather than strike out alone. Mutual funds are high-flying projects where the resources of many people are pooled together in order to purchase scaled securities. The funds will be contributed by various investors in the group in exchange for a slice of ownership in the fund. The fund has a manager, who will take the time to study the market and eventually make the best decisions for everyone in the group. While the manager makes the decisions, it will be the board who will authorize it.

In most instances, these mutual funds need to have goals. The manager is then responsible for making sure that the fund reaches those goals.

The shares that are found in a mutual fund will be bought using the fund's present Net Asset Value, or NAV. This value is derived by dividing the securities value of the total shares. Having a stake in a mutual fund is often more secure and rewarding compared to purchasing shares from a bunch of random companies. They also work well because smaller investors are able to own a portion of the value in the fund's portfolio.

Even if the investor is not able to invest a lot of money, they can join a mutual fund and increase their odds of making money. Considering most fund managers have a lot of experience in the stock market and are earning consistently high returns on the choices they make for investing, it is often safer and more profitable to use mutual funds rather than just trading on the stock market on your own.

To keep it simple, mutual funds are going to take money from many investors and pool it together. This helps give individual investors more buying power than they had on their own. The fund manager is able to choose which securities are the best for the whole company to invest in. They will work to make a profit for everyone involved in the mutual fund. The investor benefits because they get more buying power, they can earn a profit, and they automatically get diversity in their portfolio this way.

There are many types of mutual funds that you can try out. Some of the ones that you should consider are:

- Target date funds
- Smart beta funds
- Alternative funds
- Equity funds
- Sector funds
- Money market funds
- Balanced funds
- Index funds
- Fixed income
- Funds of funds

There are different reasons why you would like to purchase from a mutual fund rather than pick stocks on your own and buy them. Some of these reasons include:

- *Professional management.* Most investors do not have the information, skills, or time to invest on their own. With a mutual fund, a professional manager is going to take over and make investment decisions for you.
- *Diversification.* There is no other way to get as much diversification as quickly as possible than with a mutual fund.
- *Economies of scale.* A mutual fund is going to purchase and sell in big volumes, so they get reduced fees. They can also invest in bigger proportions compared to what a single person can do.
- *Simple.* Getting into a mutual fund only takes a few clicks to be done.
- *Lots of transparency.* Mutual funds need to meet certain regulations so you know they are safe to invest in.
- *Ease of access.* You can easily purchase or sell your mutual fund holdings on the exchange at any time.

- *Custom.* You are able to search around and find a mutual fund that aligns with your goals and with what you want to invest in.

Index Funds and ETFs

An index is a collection of securities that will represent the value of an economic sector. Investors track indices to help determine how badly or well a market sector is doing. An index fund, on the other hand, is going to be a collection of securities investments that will involve tracking market performance. Investors are going to gain any time the market goes up. These index funds are a viable option because they can offer you a lot of exposure to the market with lower expenses, compared to other options such as hedge funds.

These index funds are sometimes known as a form of passive fund management, and they will bring in more gains compared to mutual funds. Most of these index funds are going to track the S&P 500, which is the top 500 public companies in terms of market capitalization in the NASDAQ or the New York Stock Exchange.

Before you decide to purchase one of these index funds, you need to understand what the index is and then check the rate in which your index fund will replicate the gains of its index. And while this is sometimes seen as a more passive form of investing, the portfolio manager needs to figure out how to track the index to make the most money.

Now, an exchange-traded fund or ETF is going to be a collection of securities investments whose shares can be purchased or sold on the stock market at a set market price. This is similar to what you would find in a mutual fund because it tries to pool resources from many investors before investing it in the most profitable markets. The ETF needs to have a goal for investing and a sense of direction.

Most of these ETFs are only going to invest in securities, and they must make sure that they operate using the guidelines set by the SEC. As an investor, there are several types of ETFs that you can choose to invest in, including the following:

- Active or passive management

- Fixed bonds or income
- Income and dividend
- Currency
- Commodities
- International
- Sector and industry
- Broad market
- Capitalization-weighted
- Factor-based strategies
- Hedged or leveraged strategies

These ETFs are going to be listed on an exchange and you can either purchase or sell shares during trading hours. The price of the ETF is going to be determined by market forces. You can buy these ETFs through a broker at any time during normal trading hours. These are great options because they are going to promote a lot of portfolio diversification, which can really reduce your risks and increase your potential profits. The operating fees that come with these types of investments are also quite a bit lower compared to hedge funds and mutual funds. ETFs are also associated with high liquidity, making it easier to sell them if you ever decide to get out of the market.

As you can see, there are a lot of options when it comes to choosing the right investment for your needs. You should carefully consider each one to figure out which will bring you the most profits with the least amount of risk. You should also factor in your own personal trading style when you begin working with the stock market.

Chapter 3: How to Choose the Right Stock When You are Ready to Invest?

Now that we know a little more about the stock market, it is time to learn more about which stock is the best for you. There are thousands and thousands of different stocks available for you to invest in, but not all of them are going to be right for your investment. The first thing you need to do is to learn which stock is going to help you actually earn a profit on your money. Some of the ways you can tell if a stock is a right investment for you include:

Choose Stocks in a Market You Understand

The first thing you need to do when you want to purchase a stock is to find a field that you know a little bit about. With the diversity of the market, this field could be banking, energy, health care, insurance, real estate, and tech, among others.

It is easier to invest when you know about the market the stock is in. You would then have a better understanding of what drives that market, the competition in that market, and how people in that market would react when something changes. You would want to do as much research on the market as possible, even if you already have a good understanding of how it works from the beginning.

Look at the National Market

The NASDAQ and the New York Stock Exchange make up the vast majority of trading volume not just in the United States, but also in the whole world. But this does not mean that you are limited to just working with the stocks on these exchanges. You can also choose to look at some of the other exchanges throughout the world. You may find that the Japan Stock Exchange, the London Stock Exchange, the Euronext, or the Shanghai Stock Exchange have some better options for your investments.

Additionally, you may find that the current state of the economy in one country may be quite a bit different in another country. For instance, Canada may have a bull market where stock prices are increasing, while India may have a bear market where stock prices are dropping. Each country is going to be different so it is often best for you to pick stocks based on an exchange that you are quite familiar with. For most people, looking at the U.S. market is the best option.

Do You Know Much About the Company?

You can't just pick a stock because it looks like it is doing well. You need to have as much information about the company as possible before you choose to invest. Investigate and see what you can come up with. Some of the things you need to look out for when deciding whether the company is a good investment or not include:

- What the company does to make profits
- Where is the company based out of
- The industry the company is in
- The competitors of the company
- Updates on what the company is doing or is going to do in the future

This does not mean that you only have to invest in companies that you know a lot about, but it can help. If you choose to invest in a company that you are not really familiar with, then, you need to do enough research to fully understand what they are about before you purchase a stock. This information is going to be really critical when it comes to how much success you will find with this investment.

Look at the Trends for the Price

The next thing we need to look at is how the value of that stock is trending. While the market may move on an upward trend, each stock is going to have its own personal trend that you need to follow. You want to watch and see whether the price is going up or down. If you see that the price is going down, and it has been trending this way for some time, then, it may be best to find another stock to invest your money in.

These price trends can be really helpful, but you also need to take a look at how long those trends are occurring and if there were any big changes that caused them to happen. There is always a chance that the stock will go back up if it starts to decline, but this is not always the case. You will need to figure out why the price trend is going down for that company and then figure out if it is likely to go back up.

Work with Some of the Moving Averages

One method that you can work with when investing is to watch the moving average of your stock. This is going to be the series of averages of a stock's price over a long period of time. To do this, we are going to look at an example of establishing a 14-day moving average. This is so we can get a good idea of how the stock is changing, without having to be bogged down by all the ups and downs of the company.

1. To start, take a look at the closing price of the stock. Grab that number from each of the past 14 days.
2. Add those 14 closing prices together.
3. Divide the number you got in the last step by 14.
4. This gives you the full moving average.
5. Go through and get as many of these moving averages for 14 days as possible. You can compare March 1 to 14, March 2 to 15, March 3 to 16, and so on to check if there is a big change or not.

When you use as many of these moving averages you get, it helps give you a better idea of how that stock changes. Day traders are going to benefit more if they do a shorter time frame for a moving average. You can also combine some long-term and short-term averages if you need a clearer picture of how the stock has been faring in the market. This is useful for all investors who want to get an idea of how individual stocks, as well as the market, are changing over time.

Check out the Company's Relationship with Their Revenue and Their Debt

A business that is able to bring in more revenue than debt is clearly doing well. It is going to have enough funds to manage all its operations, cover expenses and debts, and pay its employees. Although the revenues of a business are important, you also have to look at the debts because if these are too large for the amount of revenue the company makes, it can spell disaster. The debts are going to include any expenses for loans to purchase new assets or to manage the salaries of the employees.

You can take a look at the gap that occurs between the debt and the revenue, and how it has changed throughout time. Financial documents from the company will reveal what was able to influence those totals and how they may change in the future.

Compare How That Stock Is Doing Compared to Other Choices You Can Make

The next thing you need to investigate is how other similar stocks are doing in the market. This gives you a yardstick to measure that stock and see if it performs in a similar or in a very different manner from other similar companies on the market. You will want to check out multiple stocks in the same field.

If you are trying to work with a retail stock, you need to check at least four retail-oriented stocks to see which is going to be the best for you. You can also take the time to look at the backgrounds of those companies to give you a better idea on how they are functional or profitable.

If you do this analysis and find that the stock is performing better than some of the others in the same industry, find out why. It may be that the company is doing something good that will keep the trend going.

But it is also possible that this was just a small change in the market and the price would not be able to last. If you find that the stock is doing poorly compared to some of its competitors in the industry, it may be better to avoid that stock, or at least consider why it is not doing the best at that time.

Each investor is going to have their own criteria when it comes to picking out the perfect stock to start their investment on. But having a list of things to check out when it comes to looking at stocks can make things easier. It helps you avoid being distracted from focusing your attention on a stock that will do well over the long term, rather than over the short term.

Chapter 4: Looking Over an SEC Report

Before we get into the specifics of joining the stock market and some of the strategies you can use, we need to take a look at the SEC reports. This is a great way to learn more about the stocks that you want to invest in. Any company that is public and has stock will need to release one of these reports each year. You can look through the data in these reports in order to find the best stocks to invest in. Let us take a look at these reports and explore what information you can find inside of it.

The Background of This Report

SEC reports are documents that all publicly traded companies need to submit to the SEC each year. These reports have been a requirement since 1933 when the Securities Act was passed following a big stock market crash a few years before. The U.S. government requires this as a way to ensure that all financial reports from these companies are specific and transparent before anyone tries to trade with them.

These reports are important to investors. They help investors make sensible decisions about the stocks and companies they want to invest in. This would help discourage investors from making a stock purchase that they do not really understand, something that was at the bottom of the big stock market crash of 1929.

By having a business share all its financial information with the public, the SEC is trying to ensure that fraudulent activities would happen less often. Every business you want to invest in will need to have these kinds of reports available.

These reports need to be detailed to help prove how much the company is worth and how they run their business. If the business fails to provide enough information in these reports, it is highly suspicious and you may want to consider investing in another company.

The 10-K Report

The first report that you can look through is the 10-K. This is just a basic document that can give you a good overview of the annual performance of a company. It will contain a lot of the information on the company, except for the electoral processes which the investor does not need to know about.

This is a vital document because it gives you a good understanding of how the business works. It helps you see how the company is running and what are its different holdings. The information you get from here can be very valuable. If you just want the basics to help compare a few companies before diving in, then, this is the report that you need to look through.

Summary of Operations

The first point you can look through in your 10-K report is the summary of operations. This is going to include a lot of different information about the company including:

- *The background of the business.* This will provide you with information on what the company does or what it sells.
- *The business strategy.* This could include information on how the business is working to move forward.
- *Information on current offerings.* This must include information on both the non-physical and physical items that the company has. It can also show any service that the company is providing outside of its products.
- *Competition points.* This section is not going to specifically name a competitor, but it will include information on how other parties in that field would offer certain services or products. This is a good place for the company to show itself as competitive and different from others on the market.
- *Research and development data.* This section should include any information on what the business is doing to find new products and make them available. It also has information on the amount of money the company spends to do this.

- *Trademarks, copyrights, patents, and licenses.* If there are any new applications for these things, they need to be included. This helps the investor to know if the company is committed, and if they are prepared in case a legal issue comes up. You may find that it is beneficial to invest in a company that cares about its efforts. There would not be a ton of information here though.
- *Foreign information.* This section means any operations that the company has outside of its base country.
- *Business seasonality.* This is going to show you when the company does a lot of its business. Some companies have more seasonal demand than others.

You can take the information on this report in order to come up with the right strategy for investing. It may tell you the best time to invest in the market, whether or not a company is doing well, or any other information you need to make informed decisions.

The Financial Outlook Information

The next thing you can look through is the financial outlook information. This is going to show any of the financial approaches that the company is currently using. The information that may be present in this part of the report will include the following:

- The net revenue the business earns from its operations
- The gross margin
- The operating income
- The costs the company spends on research and development
- The effective tax rate
- The total value of any assets the business has
- The debt the business holds
- How many employees the business has

This financial information is going to include some historic points for you to look at as well. You can see whether the business is doing better or worse because there are certain prior points to compare. An annual report usually compares its performance for the current year with the past year. This gives you important insight into the business and whether it is going to last.

The Balance Sheet

Next on the list is the balance sheet. This is going to show a lot more financial information for the shareholder. It can give them a good look into whether the company has enough revenue to handle their debts and whether or not the investor will actually be able to make anything with that company. Some of the information that needs to be included on the balance sheet include:

- *The assets the company has.* This can include both long-term and short-term assets. They include things like property, equipment, investments, accounts receivable, inventory, and cash.
- *The liabilities of the business.* This could include any debts for long loans or bonds payable, customer advances, taxes or interests, and accounts payable for the company.
- *The equity of the shareholder's.* This is going to refer to the assets minus the liabilities. It is a measure of how healthy the company is. The total focus is on what the shareholders might be able to get back if the company is liquidated and the debts are paid off.

Income Statement

The income statement is another document you can read through when you are coming up with an investment strategy. This statement is going to show all the information on what the business is earning over time. This statement will have information on at least the last three years of the business. If you can get more information, that is even better because it provides you with a great picture of where the business is going and what has happened in the past few years.

10-Q Report

The 10-Q report is going to be similar in content with the 10-K report. However, it will focus more on the quarterly results of a business. It can include information about the financial statements for the business like different expenses, taxes, operating income, and gross profits. It can also include details about any big developments that occurred in the past quarter, ongoing legal proceedings, and risk factors, and some contracts that were set up with various groups during that time. This report can be useful to look at to determine how the company is doing right now.

A delay in submitting the 10-Q or the 10-K reports could also result in noncompliance with the listing standards of the New York Stock Exchange and the NASDAQ. If a company fails to gain compliance within the allowed period, its shares could be subject to delisting.

8-K Report

The 8-K report often goes by the name of Current Report. This is a statement that the company will issue whenever they have some major event that they must tell the public about now. Sometimes this report is just going to talk about something that caused the company to grow. But sometimes it will also talk about problems that are more difficult and can be red flags when it comes to your investment. This kind of report is filed so the company can discuss any of the following:

- Bankruptcy filing
- An introduction to some key developments and issues that the shareholders need to vote on
- Any amendments to the Code of Ethics of the company
- Cases where the estimates that a business is expected to earn are dramatically altered in value. This usually happens if the value decreases.
- Any events that will make one of the company's financial obligations change
- The completion of a new and major acquisition plan

- When the company either enters or leaves a material definitive agreement
- The departure or appointment of certain company officers and directors

There are technically no limits on how many of these reports aresent out by a business. You would need to look at how the company lists them. Any company that uses these should be thorough and transparent when they publish these reports so that the investor knows what is causing the changes.

Schedule 13D

The Schedule 13D is another type of SEC filing that will cover details about who owns the shares of the company. A company needs to file this within 10 days after someone acquires five percent or more of any security. This helps other investors know how one person may be managing a lot of the shares of the company. It sometimes shows that one person is going to heavily influence that company. Some of the information that needs to be on the Schedule 13D include:

- Details on that security
- Information on the person who acquired that security. This can include the person's contact information and their background.
- The source of the funds for that transaction
- The reason that someone is acquiring these shares
- Any relationships or contracts that this investor has with others who are inside the business
- Letters and other documents that will show how the transaction occurred

This is an important document for an investor to look over because it gives a good idea on who owns the shares. If one individual or group starts taking over too much of the shares of a company, it could mean that some major changes are going to occur in the near future. You have to weigh whether this is a good thing or a bad thing before you decide to invest.

Form 144

The last form we are going to look at is the Form 144. This is going to cover how the stocks were made available to the public. This needs to be filed any time someone who is associated with the company plans to sell their stocks. This could be an important figure, such as the executive or director. This form is a simple document that is just two pages long. It needs to include the following details before being filed:

- The name of the company that issued the stock
- The title of the class of stock or security being sold
- The number of shares that are being sold at that time
- The names of any security exchanges that are being used
- How many of these shares are outstanding
- The market value of these shares
- Information on any of the other securities that the individual is selling, including any other shares that might have been sold in the past three months through them

The Form 144 needs to factor into your strategy when you look at how these shares are being made available to the public. Sometimes this kind of report is just showing that someone who works in the business is ready to retire so they sell off their shares. This usually is not a big deal and you can still get into the investment.

However, there are times when this is a sign that something big is going to happen in the business, such as someone else buying out a party of that entity. Depending on which party is involved and how that may change the business, this is definitely something that you need to watch out for and plan for before purchasing the security.

Chapter 5: How to Get into the Stock Market and Pick Out the Best Trading Platforms

No matter what kind of strategy you decide to work with, it is going to be worthless if you are also not working with the proper trading platform. This trading platform is basically the program you are going to work with in order to make your trades directly. You can usually get one of these from a banking institution or your personal broker.

The trading platform is a necessity if you are an everyday trader. It allows you to do your trades from your own home electronically, so you do not have to go down in person to get the work done. The earliest of these platforms would let you find updated information on the stock prices, while allowing you to send signals about when you want to trade. The high-speed online world has changed so much that platforms can handle these transactions immediately and you can see real-time prices. All that is needed to make this happen is an online connection.

Analytics Points

A trading platform that you choose should have various analytics that are going to make it easier for you to identify what stocks you want to work with. While you should automatically be able to find real-time charts and quotes about any stock you want with this program, you need to be aware of other things as well. Some of these include:

News Feeds Are Important

Your chosen platform needs to have some news feeds. These are going to include some reports from news organizations like Reuters and the Associated Press. This news feed is going to give you all the information that you need on everything that happens in the market. A platform can even search through the feed if you need to find a specific information on a stock. To look through the news feed, you just need the following steps:

- Look for the name of the stock you want to invest in.
- Check to see which exchange that stock is in and what symbol it uses
- Enter the content by listing it as the following: Abbreviation of exchange: symbol. This lets the program know what you are looking for.
- Check the results. These results might include details on the forecasts and even some SEC reports. Any outstanding events that need to be included will be here too.

The Right Security

You are going to be handling a lot of money through the platform. You will submit payments into the platform so you can purchase the stocks you want. And then, when you earn any profits, that money is going to come back to you as well. Depending on how much you trade, it is possible that you are going to have a lot of financial transactions.

With all of this money going back and forth, you want to make sure that your financial information is as secure as possible. If a platform has had trouble with a data breach recently, it may be best to go with someone else. Check if they have a good customer support system as well to ensure that someone will be there to help you if you have concerns with the security of your account.

Financial Points

Depending on the type of platform you choose, each one is going to have some additional financial fees that are specified by that trading platform. You need to know these fees because they are going to influence how much you will actually earn on each trade. Some of the things that you should focus on when it comes to picking out a trading platform include:

- Each platform is going to have their own fee structure for how much you will pay to do a trade. Some have a flat fee for a single trade or they may have a fee that is based on the number of shares you will purchase or sell. Sometimes the fees will end up cheaper if you do a bulk transaction.
- Options traders are going to have to pay extra for their contracts. The extra charge for each contract might not be much depending on the type of contract it is.
- An account minimum may be required in some cases. A lender may want you to keep a certain amount of money in the account before you decide to start trading. This helps them see that you are actually committed on trading on their platform. The amount is going to vary on each platform.
- Sometimes a platform will offer a special promotion. This could be a cash bonus for any qualifying deposit. You might get $100 in extra money for trading if you put in $1000 or more into the account to start.
- Each platform has their own margin rates. The margin rates offered for options might be within a few percentage points of the current stock value.

What Are Some of the Best Platforms to Trade On?

The platform that you will use is going to vary depending on what kind of trading you would like to do, how much it costs, and which one seems to be the best fit for you. There are a lot of great options, but here are some of the best:

- Ally Invest
- TD Ameritrade
- TradeStation
- Interactive Brokers
- Charles Schwab
- EOption

If you are uncertain about which of these platforms is the best one for you, consider trying a few out. You can sometimes get a sample trade so that you can mess around on the platform and find which one is the most comfortable for your needs. If you find the one that feels more natural or is easier to use than others, then go ahead and give that a try!

Chapter 6: Understanding the True Value of a Stock

As you are looking through stocks and trying to figure out which ones you want to invest in, you are also going to learn which strategy is the best for you. But sometimes it is better to think about the underlying factors of a stock. The value of the stock may not be as good as the official total says, or the stock is overvalued. Picking one of these stocks could result in you losing money when the market figures things out and the price goes down.

At the same time, a company may be doing well, but you may see that the stock price does not reflect this. This would be a good option to go with because the value is likely to go up as the market adjusts to reflect the total value of the company. You are going to need to look at several points to see how a stock is performing and if it is a good idea to go with that. Some points that you can look at include:

P/E Ratio

A good strategy to help you review the worth of the stock is knowing the price to earnings ratio, or the P/E ratio. This measurement is going to show you what investors are actually willing to spend on any given stock.

When you get a higher total here, it means investors expect to earn more over time from that option. When the total comes in low, this means the stock is undervalued. This could mean that this stock is an intriguing choice to go with. If you want to get this ratio, you need to do the following:

1. Take the current price of the stock.
2. Divide that number by the earnings per share, or EPS. If you do not have this number, the EPS is the net income divided by the outstanding shares.
3. This will give you the P/E ratio.

The total value that you get for the P/E ratio refers to how much value the market is currently placing on the stock. When the ratio is higher, the stock market is going to value it more. When the market values it more, it means this is a stock that people want to purchase.

Let us look at an example of how this works. Looking at a stock, you may see that it has a market price of $26.26. Meanwhile, it has an EPS of $2.28. This is based on a net income of $697 million divided by 304.57 million outstanding shares of the company.

When you divide the value of the stock by the EPS, you are going to end up with a total of $11.52. This means that the average investor is willing to pay $11.52 for every dollar that the company earns. This is a cheap total because it shows that not too many investors are willing to go with this stock. If the P/E ratio is low, it shows that the stock is worth investing in if you want to find something less expensive on the market.

If you look at the company and see that they are losing money, there is going to be an N/A where the P/E ratio should be. You can technically go through and calculate a negative ratio and show that this company is losing money. It is often easier to use N/A to show that investors are not going to gain much when they invest in the company, because the company is not earning much and cannot put a number there.

Some investors still choose to go with this kind of stock because they can get it for a lower price. It all depends on the reason why the company is losing money. If they are losing because they went through an expansion, then, the number will go up in the near future, and it may be a good idea to invest while the stock is cheaper.

Now, what is the optimal P/E ratio that you want to trade on? It is hard to know whether a stock has a good P/E ratio. Each industry is going to be different. In the technology sector, a P/E ratio of 25 is a good option, but in some other industry, a ratio of 14 can be better. You need to experiment and see what looks the most enticing for you.

A Note About Inflation

Before we move on, it is important to talk about inflation a bit when you are doing the P/E ratio. This measurement is often going to be a bit lower whenever the rate of inflation is high. This is because the earnings of the business are going to be skewed as inflation rises. It usually takes more than a few months for this inflation rate to make a big difference, but you do want to consider this in your calculations.

Price/Earnings Growth Ratio

The next type of measurement that you should look into when reviewing the true value of a stock is the price/earnings growth, or PEG, ratio. This is important because it is going to provide you with a measure of whether a particular stock is underpriced or if it is undervalued or not. It may also let you know if you are getting a huge bargain when you purchase a stock. You can measure the PEG ratio through the following steps:

1. Calculate the P/E ratio of the stock using the method we talked about before.
2. Divide this number by the annual EPS growth.

Let us look at an example of this. Say a business has a share price of $50 and an EPS of $4. The total may have gone up to $6 this year. Therefore, we are going to calculate the P/E ratio by diving 50 by 6, which gives us the answer of 8.33. Now, divide those earnings by taking 6 and dividing it by 5 while subtracting 1. This gives you an answer of 0.5 or 50 percent. The EPS growth is going to give you 50 percent. Divide the 8.33 by 50 and you get a PEG of 0.166.

The PEG might sound minimal, but this means that the stock is trading on a big discount compared to how much it is growing. This means that you could purchase the stock for way less than it is worth and as the company grows, you will make more and more. Over time, the value may help you get a great deal because the company is stable.

The point of doing the PEG is to give you a good idea of what you can expect from a stock that you might hold onto for some time. It shows that there is an upward trend in that stock. If you have a stock that has a favorable PEG, you might be more willing to hold onto it for longer because it is a great deal and will keep growing in the future.

The Price/Sales Ratio

The next strategy that you can choose to work with is the price/sales ratio or the PSR. The reason you may want to use this one is because it compares the value the company's stock to its revenue. The stock of a company that has a good amount of revenue shows that the business is active and that is likely to stay around for some time. The steps that you can take to analyze the PSR are:

1. Find the total number of the available outstanding shares.
2. Add the sales totals for each of the past 12 months.
3. Divide those sales totals by the number of shares.
4. Divide the current value of the share by the numbers you got in the third step.
5. This gives you the PSR based on how the past year of trading has gone for the business.

You can also change this up and replace the sales totals for the past 12 months with sales for the ongoing fiscal year if you want. This will give you an answer that is more relevant, but it will still probably be similar. Numbers for the current fiscal year can be used to help with this forecast. The measurement from the past 12 months is going to be more analytical, allowing you to see what has changed over time with the business.

If you see that the PSR is low, this means you can purchase the stock at a good discount. This shows how the company has a low cost compared to the revenues it is earning. If you want to purchase a stock, now is the perfect time to do it. This one is a good indicator because it is based on the sales of the company.

The business is going to have a hard time altering its sales totals compared to any estimates that the accounting team may try to showcase. The sales totals are going to be more stable and will work through cycles that change throughout the year. You can sometimes make a prediction about it, but you will not be able to fake it or make major changes to it like some other estimations you can do for a business.

Analyze the Book Value of the Company

When you are trying to figure out the true value of a stock, you may want to spend some time looking at its book value. This is going to refer to the value of the assets that are in the stock, minus any liabilities and other intangible assets that the company is holding on to.

Simply put, the book value is going to refer to the value that an asset holds on the company's balance sheet. It will measure out what the shareholder will receive if the company has to liquidate tomorrow. This is going to be an estimate and you probably should not base all of your trades on it. The book value is something that you can explore though. The most important point about the book value is that it is going to measure how a business will function. A business that has a better book value should not be one that has enough assets to keep it operational.

There are some issues that come with using this strategy because the book value may not be the best option every time. A business that is growing very quickly may not have an accurate book value because it is trying to accumulate more assets and wants to make some changes in the way it operates. Businesses that do not have a lot of physical assets also may not score high on this strategy.

In some cases, the intangible assets of a company could be a big problem. The reputation of a business may go through some damage or there could be a controversy or legal issue against one of the products or services that it offers. This would be hard to show in the book value of the company. Some of these, such as the reputation of the company, can be repaired over time, but for the short term, they could put some dents in how well a stock does.

The book value works the best if it is helping you when you are not sure whether a stock is the right one for you. Sometimes it can show you more information than the others. But this one does run into some issues that the others do not, and it is best to be careful about relying on this one on its own.

To make sure you are picking out a stock that is a good one and is offered at a deal, you may want to utilize a few of these strategies at once. This helps you see if the stock is really a good one to go with or not. If the company is strong on several of these strategies, then, it may be a good one to invest your money in. If it has mixed reviews between the strategies, you may want to reconsider using it or not. But if it fails on more than one, it is a good sign that you should stay away and not use it at all.

Chapter 7: How to Make Money in the Stock Market Using a Fundamental Analysis

A fundamental analysis is one of the first strategies that you can consider using. It is the study of the financial data of a company. The aim with this one is to determine the financial health and performance of a particular company. You are also trying to use this information to project whether the company is going to be weak or strong in the future. The fundamental analysis is a critical exercise because it helps investors decide whether the company is a good idea to invest in over the long term.

You should use this kind of analysis, at least in part, in any valuation you do on a security. Most investors tend to forget to use this one, but it can really help you find out if a security is as strong as it looks. You will look through several key metrics including projected future growth, interest rates, profit margins, and income to determine if this is the right choice for you.

Fundamental analysis is basically looking at the company and figuring out how the company is doing regardless of the price of the stock. Do they make good profits? Do they have a good plan for the future? Is their reputation good? Are they working on something that will really benefit them in the future? If these are all true and yet the stock is still lower than market rates, it may show that this is a good investment to get in to.

It is important that you have a few tools to help you do a fundamental analysis so that you can look past the face value. Some of the factors that you are going to use for this analysis include:

- *Earnings per share.* What percentage of the profits goes to the shareholders?
- *Price to earnings ratio.* What is the current share price to its EPS?
- *Dividend Yield.* What are the yearly dividends that are paid out compared to the prices of the stock?

- *Dividend payout ratio.* What is the amount of dividends paid to the shareholders compared to how much the company makes?
- *Price to book ratio.* What is the book value of the stock when compared to its market value?
- *Price to sales ratio.* What is the share price compared to the revenue of the corporation?
- *Projected earnings growth*: By what percentage is the stock going to grow within a year?
- *Return on equity.* What is the company's return on equity? You can find out by dividing the net income of the company by the stockholder's equity.

The fundamental analysis can often be a great way to figure out if the company is offering shares at a discount compared to their worth. There are plenty of great stocks out there offering great dividends and good returns on investment, but other stockholders may undervalue them or may not even know them at all. You can use a fundamental analysis to help you find these stocks and get the most out of them.

Chapter 8: How to Recognize Patterns in a Stock

Some of the most popular strategies that you are going to use in the stock market will focus on patterns. These are cases where something is likely to change with a stock within a given time. Patterns can show how the stock price is moving, while still giving you a signal that something else will likely happen. There are a lot of different patterns you can work with. It is sometimes easy to figure them out once you learn how the stock is evolving. You can use these patterns to your advantage by having them help you plan your strategies for when to enter and exit a trade, or when figuring out the kinds of trades you should make. Let us take a look at a few of these and see what needs to happen so we can recognize some of the patterns.

Continuation or Reversal?

The most important thing you need to notice about these patterns is that there are two forms, and they often mean very different things when it comes to reading them.

- *Reversal.* This is when a current trend is starting to end. So, the stock may have spent some time going up, but with a reversal, it is going to start going down.
- *Continuation.* This shows that the price changes in the stock are going to continue along, even when the pattern is finished. The pattern may be a brief occurrence, but then, the stock is going to continue on unabated when that is done.

These points can be used to help determine how you should trade a stock. You might consider purchasing a stock to sell later, or you could put in a call or put option depending on how you see that stock moving now and in the future. Either way, you can always invest in a stock, no matter whether it moves up or down in value.

One thing that you will notice with continuations and reversals is that they tend to go on for a long time. It is difficult for an investor to look at a trend and know how long it will last, but it is likely that the current trend will keep going on for some time.

Pennant

The pennant is a good pattern to look out for when trying to pick out a stock. This is going to be one of the continuation patterns that show how a stock can keep growing in value. At this point, the stock is going to appear to be struggling, trying to move up or down. But then, after some time, the stock is going to break out of the pennant and will keep moving toward the same position it had at the start. Some of the things this pennant can reveal to an investor include:

1. The value of your stock is either going to start decreasing or increasing sharply. The change may be the stock losing or gaining a few percentage points of value. The change should be noticeable, no matter how valuable it is.
2. The value should then start to go in the opposite direction. So, it is going to slowly decrease after a sizeable increase, or it may go the other way around as well.
3. After some time, the values of the drops or the rises in the stock will start to minimize a bit. The stock might end up changing by just a few pennies in value after each candlestick. Sometimes the total volume or the range in which the stock changes value may be minimal.
4. Next, you are going to notice that the stock has little, and sometimes no change in value.
5. The pennant is going to end whenever the stock suddenly breaks out and sees a bit increase or decrease in its value. This should be a full continuation of what the stock experienced earlier in the game.

The layout of the pennant is going to let you know that the value of that stock is either stabilizing or it is about to break out. When the trading volume and the change in value shrink to almost nothing, it is a sign that something is going to happen soon. Sometimes, you will see that the value of that stock will go either up or down, depending on how the pennant started.

You will want to enter into this pennant when you notice that the changes that occur in each wave going down are very low totals. You can then watch to see how the pennant ends up being formed and check to see how the stock will break out. Then, place a stop-loss order on the opposite end of the trend to help provide a safeguard in case things do not go the way you want.

Bearish or Bullish?

A pennant has the power to be either bearish or bullish in value. When the pennant is a bullish one, it starts with a bit of a rally. The stock price is going to go up in the beginning, and then, it stabilizes. When the pennant has time to form, the stock is then going to move back up in value.

A bearish pennant is going to feature a price that will drop quite a bit before the pennant forms. The price may look like it is going up for a bit, and then,it will see a decline in value when the pennant ends.

Strategies to Help You Use a Pennant

There are a few strategies that can be useful when you are relying on a pennant. These include the following:

Watch for how changes in your candlestick patterns are going to vary when the pennant starts moving forward. Sometimes a majority of sticks in the pennant will end up going upwards or downwards. Either way, you might want to get into the trade after you see the pennant has formed all the way. You can also try to make some micro-transactions that last for a few minutes depending on where that pennant is flowing. It can be difficult though to determine how long the waves will move along and how many of the down or up candlesticks will be formed at this time.

Next, you can consider looking for as many of these pennants in a stock as possible. If you see many pennants there, it gives you a good idea on the sentiment around that stock. You may see that a bullish pennant is becoming bigger in size. This also shows that investors are liking that stock and are willing to invest in it.

Trade during the upside parts of the stock if possible. When you trade during this part, it helps you to identify some points where the value of the stock will probably increase in a short amount of time. This is going to work just for a brief time before something starts to shrink in value.

See if there are any big outliers to the pennant. This could be something like one stick in the middle of the pennant that is longer or larger than any others. This outlier often shows that there is some uncertainty in the stock. When you see the outlier starts to move down, this shows that the potential for an increase is not as strong as it should be.

And finally, you should look at how long this pennant might be moving. Sometimes the pennant is strong to last for a few weeks or more, but usually, this just lasts for a few hours. This is because many people watch the stock market and they are going to respond pretty quickly to any changes that come in the stock. They may notice that a stock is trending up and is stable, so they may acquire it before the value bursts up again.

The Wedge Pattern

The next pattern you can watch out for is the wedge. This one is going to have some similarities with the pennant, but with a different kind of shape. The wedge will be a pattern when the price wave is going to reverse. The range in the price of the stock is going to narrow after some time and then the stock will break out and either move down or up after the wedge is done.

So, how is the wedge different than the pennant? A wedge is organized based on the differences between stock prices that are in a specific range. There are three main types of wedges that you can watch out for.

- *Rising Wedge.* This is when the lows and the highs of this pattern keep on moving up. You can tell when this wedge is rising that the stock price is going to start a new downward trend. You need to sell your stock when the low on a rising wedge breaks beyond the lower bar because the stock is going to experience an even bigger decline soon.
- *Falling wedge.* The falling wedge is going to be the opposite of what we saw with the rising wedge. This is when the lows and the highs for the stock continue to decrease. You will want to purchase the stock when it breaks out from the top part of your wedge.
- *Symmetrical wedge.* This kind of wedge is designed in a way that is very similar to a pennant. So if you have used a pennant, this one should look familiar. However, you will see that the narrowing of your gap is not going to be as close as you see with a pennant. You will be able to check and see if the wedge is going up or down by looking where it began on the chart.

The Cup and Handle Pattern

A cup and handle price pattern is going to look just like a cup in the shape of a "U" with a handle that goes slightly down. The right hand of the pattern is going to show a low trading volume and can be as short as just seven weeks or as long as up to 65 weeks.

A stock that is showing this kind of pattern is working to test out old highs. It is going to put selling pressure for any investor who purchased at those levels. This selling pressure is going to make price consolidation a tendency toward a downward trend for four days to four weeks. When that is done, it is going to advance even higher. This is considered a bullish pattern and it can help you figure out the best times to get into the market and make money.

When looking at your chart pattern, you want to make sure you go with a cup that has more of a "U"-shaped bottom than one that is sharper and looks like a"V."The cup and the handle should not be too deep as well. The volume should decrease as the stock price declines, and it should remain lower than the average you see in the base of the bowl. This helps you see the right time to make a purchase of the stock because you will able to make the most money.

To trade in this kind of pattern, you can place a stop buy order that is just a little bit about the upper trend line you see with the handle. Order execution is then only going to happen if you see this stock break that pattern. Traders may experience some excess slippage with this pattern and if you do an aggressive entry, you may enter a false breakout.

In addition, you can wait and see if the price closes above the upper trend of the handle and then, put a limit order above that breakout level. You can then attempt to get an execution if the price does retrace. This one is not always the best because you risk missing out on a trade if your pattern keeps on advancing and it does not pull back the way you want.

Head and Shoulders Pattern

You can also work with the head and shoulders pattern. This is a chart formation that is going to look like a baseline that has three peaks. Your two outer ones will be very similar in height and the middle one is going to be the highest. These are going to form when the price of the stock starts to rise. There are three main parts that come with the head and shoulders pattern:

- After a bullish trend is done, the price is going to rise to a peak before declining to form a new trough.
- The price is going to rise again in order to make a big peak. This one is going to be larger than the first one, sometimes by quite a bit. Then, it will decline again.

- The price is going to rise again, but this one will not go above like what you saw in the first peak and then, it will decline a little more.

This is often seen as a tug of war between investors and buyers. Whether the price of that stock ends up going down or up, it is going to be the result of how many investors or how many buyers there are. Those who believe that the price of that stock will go up are the bulls and those who think it will go down are the bears. If more of the shareholders are bears, then, the price will go down. But if more are bullish, then, the price is going to go up.

Triangles

Another pattern that you can explore is a triangle. This is going to be a continuation pattern, though there are times that it can end up turning into a reversal pattern. The triangle develops when the price changes in the stock are going to narrow. These steps show you exactly how this triangle pattern can get started:

1. A triangle is going to begin right when the stock heads up or down in value over a few trading periods.
2. The stock will start to go back to the opposite direction. This is going to form the line that is responsible for the other part of your triangle.
3. Your stock is going to move back and forth. The differences between these points will be smaller when the stock starts to move.
4. Eventually, the triangle is going to be formed. You will then need to be on a lookout for a breakout, which is when the stock will keep moving in the same direction that it did when the triangle started.

This is a good way for you to figure out when you should get into a trade. If you notice that a triangle is ready to start, you should watch and see which direction the trend is going. In most cases, the trend, after the triangle is done, will continue in the same direction as it started. Once the lines start forming, get in on the lower part of the triangle to get a better price for the stock and watch as the price starts to go back up. If you get in at a good time, you will be able to make a good profit on the work.

Chapter 9: When Should I Purchase Long and Sell Short?

One thing that you are going to hear a lot when you get into the stock market is to buy long or sell short. But as a beginner, these terms may be a little bit hard to understand. This chapter is going to explore these topics and what they can mean to your trading strategy.

You should buy long at any time you feel that the stock will grow more in value. It is going take more time to get a profit from your trades if you opt to buy and sell stock in the same day, but the potential for real gains are going to be greater with this method.

Then, you would want to sell short when you notice your market is falling. You want to try to sell the shares at a higher price, and then, purchase them back again at a lower price. This is different from when the long-trade requires you to actually acquire and hold on to the shares. We will explain these a bit more as this chapter goes on.

Trading in the stock market can take some time to get used to. You want to make sure you are always picking the right stocks and that you get in and out at the best times to make a profit. This chapter is going to show you some of the tips that you need to make this happen.

If you are looking at conventional wisdom, it suggests for you to buy long any time you see the stock price moving up, and then, sell short when you see the stock moving down. But there are often more variables at play when you actually get into the stock market, and we are going to take a look at how some of these will affect your decisions.

Investing with a Long Trade

First, we are going to take a look at a long trade. This is when you keep the trade for a period of time, which is something that you would not do if you want to be a day trader. Sometimes a long trade will be necessary to make money because there is a high potential for the value of the stock to go up. You need to watch for how the stock rises in value and how it moves in an upward line over time. More importantly, you have to look at what the future may hold for that stock.

You should stick with your long trade any time you want to limit your losses from trading right then and there. You can also use it if you are not interested in getting yourself into a margin deal. Working with a straightforward trade is often the best because it allows you to work with your own funds. Leveraging and other options can add to your profits, but they do put you at a risk of losing a lot of money as well.

Sometimes a stock is going to become more valuable over time because the company is strong. Trading long can be key to a big profit if you pick the right company. This can happen because the business is strong enough that its demand is going to last for a long time, or because it can consistently grow.

For example, Netflix is a good choice to go with for a long trade. Most people see Netflix as a way to stream or rent movies, series, and other original programming. Netflix started trading on the NASDAQ at the beginning 2017 with its stock worth $130. By the end of 2017, the stock rose to $200 as the company expanded its portfolio.

The key to finding a good company is to see the stock progressively growing. It can take some time, but you will make a lot of profits over time. You can also check how the business is able to sustain its growth. No matter what industry you are in, there are always going to be some new threats that can make it very hard for an investment to stay afloat. You need to make sure your chosen company is able to handle this.

Investing in a Short Trade

Another move that you can go with is a short trade. This is when you are going to sell shares that you borrow at a given time, and then, buy them back at any time that the market falls, all while making a profit. To do a short trade, you are going to have to pay a commission. If you borrowed shares at $50 each and then sell them at $80, you can make a profit of $30. However, you have to pay some commission on that profit. It is also possible that after you borrow the stocks, their value will go down and you will not make any profit from it.

A short trade is best when you have done enough research on the stock to know how it behaves. You need to look at how the stock has changed and how long you plan to borrow those stocks. You also need to know that sometimes the short sale will last for a few hours or a few weeks depending on your position.

Some investors wrongly assume that selling short is like doing a put option. But a short sale is going to include the actual sales of a business. You could end up losing a lot more money with this option if you are unable to match with the market the right way. A put option has the added benefit of being able to end the contract before your chosen date. Selling short, however, does not allow this. It becomes way riskier to go with this option compared to some of the other ones.

These are just a few of the options that you can go with when it comes to you selling short or buying long. Each trade is going to be a little bit different, so make sure to check each one out and see how they work for your needs. You need to really look into the stock and consider how each one is traded, what may happen according to the patterns that you see, and make sure you can actually earn a profit.

Chapter 10: Planning Limit or Stop Orders

Although all the patterns we have discussed in this guidebook are great to use, you never want to assume that a pattern is always going to move the way you think. Sometimes, false signals are going to develop and even a pattern that looks strong can go the opposite way you want. When your money is at risk, you also want to make sure that you are able to limit your losses. With the stock market, there is a solution that you can use to make that happen.

To help limit your losses and help plan your own stock strategies, you can try using stop orders. These are the orders that will work to help limit how much you will lose during the trade and can make your profits bigger. By adding one of these stop orders, you are telling your broker that you want that stop to happen at a certain point in time.

For these though, you are going to involve the market price. Instead of telling your broker to get out in two weeks, you will tell them to get out when the stock reaches a certain price. If the stock never gets to that point, you will stay in the market and make a good profit. But if the stock goes the opposite way you have planned, this helps keep your losses down to a minimum.

Probably, the best reason to consider doing a stop order is that it will make sure you get your emotions out of the game. One problem that a beginner may encounter when they get started with the stock market is that they let their emotions take over. They will get too involved in the trade and make bad decisions in the hopes of earning more profits. For example, they might stay in the market for too long that they end up losing money. Or, they stay in the market even when they start losing money in the hopes of getting it back. When you work with the stop order from the start, you can avoid these emotional issues and actually keep your investment going strong.

Stop Orders

A stop order is going to be done on a trade that is executed up to a specific total. The target price that you want the trade to move is going to become your stop price. Let us say you are working with a stock that can trade at $20. You could have a stop order in place by telling your broker to sell that stock when it reaches $17. The order will be kept in place by your broker. If your stock gets to $1, the trade ends.

This can help you keep the stock where you want it. It can also help you avoid losing so much money. With that stop order, you will get out of the market when it reaches $17. Even if the stock keeps going down to reach $10,you at least got out with a minimal amount of loss. But if you forgot to put that stop order in place, you may be stuck with a bigger loss.

A stop order can come in handy when you want to ensure you will earn a profit as well. You could purchase a stock at $15 and then, put a stop order in place for $19. When the stock reaches $19, you will sell and make the profit. It is possible that the stock will go back up or go even higher, but there is also a chance that the stock will go lower right away. This helps ensure that you will at least get some profits.

When you look at your graphs, you should be able to see some general trends in the stock you want to work with. You can look at these patterns and determine your stop orders based on that information. That way, you can maximize your profits as much as possible, without having to worry about losing money in the process.

Trailing Stops

Another option you can work with is a trailing stop. This is where you are going to be right behind the market price, but you will make sure that it still has a fixed amount that goes with it. This works well for any stock that is increasing in value. This can also be a very good moveto benefit from the possible gains that come from it. Let us look at an example of a trailing stop and how you would use it when trading.

- You have a stock that has its market value at $30. You may choose to put a trailing stop of $27 on this stock so you have a $3 difference between the stop and the market value.
- When the stock goes up, say to $35, your trailing stop will then move up to $32. In this case, if the stock price goes back down, you will get out at $32 and still make a profit.
- Even if the stock dips down to $33 and then back up to $34, your trailing stop will stay in place. It will only go up and not down, helping you to actually make a profit.
- The stock would go down to $32 after some time. Then, the trailing stop is executed and the trade is complete.

If you did this trade, you would make a profit of $2 on each share. This may not be a huge amount, but it still resulted in a profit and helped you earn money on the trade.

Stop and Reverse

Another option that you can choose is the stop and reverse order. This is a strategy where you take that stop order and place it at a certain point for loss. When this point is reached and the first order is attained and executed, another new order will be placed. This one is going to be a reverse of what you did on that original order. This can be used if you feel your stock will still go up in value. With this strategy, you will most likely do two separate orders to make it happen.

This is the strategy you would choose to go with if the stock has been identified as the one that will go up. You may be able to notice an upward pattern to help you forecast that the stock will go up. You can then work with your broker to set a special order to handle this strategy. If the stock does not end up increasing, then, you have taken a big risk on this strategy and you can lose a lot of money. Be careful when you choose this option.

Limit Orders

The limit order will be executed as soon as specific conditions or terms are met. The focus on this is to have the minimum and maximum orders for your trade all in line, and they will only happen when certain conditions are met. While the stop order is going to concentrate more on selling at a specific total, you can have a limit order that talks about multiple values. Here's an example of how you would do a limit order:

1. You would place a limit order on some stock that is trading right now at $15.
2. You would then place a limit order. This is where you would establish a limit of $13. This shows that you are not willing to pay more than $13 to purchase that stock.
3. You can then also set how many shares you are willing to purchase once the stock reaches that $13 mark.
4. At times, you may already own the stock when it is at $15. You can also establish a limit order to help here. You would simply set it to sell the stock at $18. If it suddenly jumps to $20, the limit order would still sell at that point and you would just make more profits.

Now, while these limits and stop orders are really nice and can help protect your investment, they are not a license for you to set up the trade and then forget all about it when the money comes rolling in. They are there to help add some safeguards, but you still need to be an active investor to get the most out of them and to protect your money.

Remember that a computer platform and a brokerage can only go so far when it comes to keeping these limits in check. Sometimes the platform that you are using is going to miss the signals that state on how an order should be executed. This is a big problem that could keep an investment from being managed the way you want.

This is especially important when you are working in a really volatile market. Things can change quickly. If the platform does not do your orders at the right times, you could end up losing more money than you planned. Being an active participant, especially if you are doing some short-term trades, can be the best way to protect your money, no matter which strategy you are trying to use.

Chapter 11: How Do I Purchase Stocks on a Margin?

There are times when you want to get in on a good trade, but you find that you do not have the money, or at least enough money, to execute that trade. In some cases, your broker may be willing to allow you to trade on a margin. Buying on a margin is a pretty simple concept. You are going to borrow money from the broker in order to do the trade that you want. This money can be used to purchase more shares or an expensive stock that you could not do so before.

Buying on the margin can be a really great way to get into more trades, but it can be risky as well. In fact, it is so risky that there are many brokers who will not allow this kind of strategy unless you have worked with them for a long time, and on many trades, in the past. Let us look at some of the specific rules that come with margin trading so you have a better understanding of how it works.

- To start, you need to work with your broker to get a margin account. This means you usually have to apply for the account. Your margin account is going to be different from your cash account.
- You will need to sign a margin agreement with your broker. The terms of this agreement can include information about how much of a margin you can trade and at what rate.
- You can make a trade if you are approved. An example of this is having $20,000 in the margin account. Then, you see a stock worth $400 a share. You might ask to purchase 100 shares, but that would require you $40,000.
- After you make this trade, the amount of money in your regular account will go toward the cost while the rest is a loan from the broker.
- You need to pay back the value of that loan at some point. This often includes interest at the margin rate. If you fail with the trade, you will still have to pay that loan back. If the stock does well, you can sell it, pay back the loan, and still take a profit. It does, however, make things a bit trickier to accomplish.

- You also need to have your margin totals in place. Your margin account could have certain limits on the amount you are allowed to borrow at a given time.

The Margin Rate

The margin rate is basically the interest your broker is going to charge on the loan they give you. The broker gets to determine how much they want to charge for the margin rate. If they charged 7 percent on that $20,000 loan, then, you would have to pay back $1,400 in interest on the margin trade. Some brokers will charge even more and they might even depend on how much you deposited into your account. Make sure you fully realize the margin rate and how much it will cost you before getting into one of these trades. Since you are borrowing money and starting a loan with a high interest rate, you do not want to get into something that kind of looks good or might be fun, because it could end up costing you quite a bit.

Strategies to Help with Margin Trading

Margin trading can be a way to make more money. But for the most part, it should only be done after you have a lot of experience with trading in the stock market. The potential for profit grows, but the margin that comes with these trades can make a loss so much worse. If you decide to trade on the margin, there are a few different strategies that you can use to make it more profitable for you. These include:

- *Keep the margins small.* Just because you have the option to trade twice the money does not mean you should do it. The smaller the margin, the less risk you are going to carry on that trade. Consider coming up with most of the money, and then, add a bit of the margin to make the trade stronger.
- *Look for the stop orders.* These stop orders are even more important if you are a margin trader. You can use these stop orders to keep the losses down.

- *Avoid speculation.* Margin trading can make it really easy to become a speculator. But as soon as you do that, you are going to lose a lot of money. Speculation is very problematic because it brings emotions back into the game and can make it hard for you to make smart decisions when trading.
- *High rewards also mean you run into higher risks.* Even though you have the opportunity to trade on the margin and make more money, it still carries a lot of risks. The risk is always greater when you add in more reward to the equation. You are working with more shares and adding more money, along with interest, which makes it really easy to lose much when you do this option. You need to think carefully about whether trading on the margin is worth the time, effort, and the risk that comes with it.

Trading on the margin can help increase your purchasing power. If you see a great trade and are certain that it will yield high profits, this can then be a way for you to jump onto that trade and make a lot of money even if you still have to pay off the loan at the margin rate. But new traders need to be careful when utilizing this option because there are also a lot of risks associated with it. Have a solid strategy and repayment plan in place in case things go wrong, and make sure that you are picking the best stocks for your needs.

Chapter 12: Other Strategies to Help You Make a Profit in the Stock Market

In addition to some of the options we have talked about, there are also a number of other choices you can make when picking out the right strategy for your needs. We are going to look at some of these other strategies that you can consider to get the most out of your investing time.

Day Trading

The first option is day trading. This method of trading is when you purchase a stock and sell it within the same day. Sometimes you will only hold onto the stock for a few minutes or hours. As long as you purchase and sell the stock within the same day, you are doing day trading. When you do all these small trades, you are able to take advantage of some of the small variations that happen each day with the stock. Even a stable stock or one that is going on an upward trend can have some fluctuations when you look at it each day. A day trader tries to take advantage of this.

The goal of day trading is to purchase the stock when it is below the market average. You will be able to find the market average by looking at charts and other data on a company. You will find that low point and make a purchase. You will keep watching the market and will wait until that stock gets to market value or above. Then, you will trade the stock out and keep the profit. The lower you can purchase the stock and the higher you can sell it in that time period, the more money you can make.

Now, it is unlikely that you will make a lot of money on each individual trade when you are doing day trading. This is because there are only small movements in the market and you will probably not see a big change in either direction in one day. But the point is that making a lot of smaller trades during the day or during the week will add up to a lot of money. When working with day trading though, you must remember that there will be broker fees each time you buy or sell a stock. These fees need to be added in to figure out if you are really making a good profit.

Swing Trading

For some investors, day trading is going to be a little bit restrictive. You have to spend all day watching the market and then, must make the trades very quickly. This is the one that most investors are going to save for when they have some expertise on the market.

Swing trading can come in and solve this problem though. It allows you to have a little more time of usually up to two weeks. You will purchase the stock, often right before a major news announcement is going to be released, and then, sell it within a few weeks after the stock goes back up. This gives you a little more leeway when it comes to how long you hold onto the stock, but it is geared toward helping you make money now rather than later in the form of dividends.

A swing trader will also concentrate efforts on looking through a technical analysis because they are able to use this information to guess what changes may occur in the near future. They may see that a stock is undervalued, but there is something that is going to raise that stock up in the next few weeks. They will purchase the stock while the prices are low, but when that big event occurs, they will be then able to capitalize on it. The fundamentals are not all that important in this option because you are more concerned about the big changes that will occur in the next few weeks compared to what will happen to the stock over a long time.

Value Investing

Many individuals who get into the stock market like the idea of value investing. The investor who chooses this strategy is looking for any stock that has a lot of strong fundamentals, such as a good amount of dividends, a good book value, earnings, and cash flow. Then, the investor can compare the market price of those stocks to the fundamentals you were calculating. In some cases, the value of the stock is going to be less than what it should be and purchasing the stock at that time means you got a hold of an amazing deal on your investment.

Now, before you choose to go with value investing, you must understand that there is a difference between a junk stock and value investing. Just because a stock is low in price does not mean that it is undervalued and will be able to grow. There are some stocks that keep a low price because they are worthless and are not attached to a good company. These stocks could be worth very little because the company does not have a good debt-to-income ratio or has a bad management.

The value stocks are different. These are the ones that have good earning potential, low debt, and are able to pay dividends to their shareholders. However, there is something that is going on in the market that results to the stock being sold for less than their value. At some point, the market will get better or the people will gain more trust in it and the value will go up for these stocks. This will not happen if you work with junk stocks.

With value investing, you are going to buy the business rather than the stock. They are going to take a look at how the company runs and decide if they want to invest. They will not look at any of the external factors that affect the company, such as a bad economy, but they are instead going to focus on the underlying worth of the company and see if it may go back up at some time.

Technical Analysis

Another option that you can choose to go with is a technical analysis. Now, there are some people who are not all that fond of using the idea of value investing. They do not like how it assumes that a stock is underpriced. Instead, they figure that the market price for the stock is what the consumer or the investor is already willing to pay, regardless of the fundamental analysis of that company. Others like this option because it gives them a way to find great deals on a company that they would not be able to invest in without this method.

A technical analyst is going to spend some of their time looking at past trading activity, along with some of the price changes that have occurred with a stock, to see whether the security is strong and how it is going to behave in the future. They are not really going to worry about the value of the company and they do not care at all about whether the company is undervalued. They just look at the charts and figure out where the stock is going in the near future.

If you decide to do a technical analysis of your stock, you need to be able to forecast the way the price is going to move. This can often be determined by the supply and demand of that stock or other security at that time. You will often figure this out by looking at the past prices of the stock, but other times you may want to include figures about volume or interest as well.

Most of the other methods that we have talked about in this guidebook are going to use a technical analysis, including all of those that rely on charts and patterns to help you get the right stock. There are a lot of different technical indicators that you can follow to make it super easy to forecast where a stock price is going. Some will simply look at the current trend of the market. Some will try to see how strong that trend is to determine if it is going to continue in the future.

As a technical analyst, you need to spend time looking at a ton of graphs, not just about the stock you are interested in purchasing, but also for the industry and even the market. This helps you look at the history of the market and better determine how it will go in the future. These patterns are going to give you a good idea of how the security is going to go in the future. You can then make your trades based on that information.

To make your technical analysis work, you need to be good at reading graphs and understanding how the market works. Some of the things that this kind of analysis is going to entail include:

- Gathering graphs and charts about the market and about your chosen stock
- Watching the news to see if there are any predicted changes in the market
- Recognizing trends in the market as well as with your stock to see what may happen in the future
- Making accurate predictions based on this research

A technical analysis is a bit different from the fundamental analysis we talked about earlier. It is meant to look at how the market, as well as the chosen stock, are doing right now price-wise and can make it easier to determine when you should get into trading for the most profits.

All of these strategies can work well to help you when you start investing. The most important part is to learn how to use each one, and then, stick with it when you are in the middle of a trade. If you are able to do all that, you are sure to see some great profits with your investing.

Position Trading

This is another strategy you can choose when you plan to stay in the market for a longer period of time. If you want to do short-term trades, pick day trading or swing trading. Many traders like to go with position trading because it allows them to stay with the same stocks and just keep up with the market, rather than having to switch all the time.

The reason many beginner traders like to go with position trading is because it gives them more time to focus and watch the trends in the market before they make their decisions to either purchase or sell a stock. They are not rushed into the position either way, and they can sometimes wait out the ups and downs of that particular stock.

When you decide to enter into a position trade, you need to take the time to look at your charts. You cannot just enter it and walk away for a few years. You still need to take care of your investment and watch it grow. You will need to watch the weekly and monthly charts because these will help you to make the important decisions that your investment needs.

The good news about the position trading option is that you do not have to worry about the short-term changes that occur in the stock as much as other options do. You can hold onto the position as long as that negative trend reverses itself. You can ride it out, wait until the price goes back up, and then, make a profit on that investment. This takes out some of the worry and stress that can come with investing, which is why many beginners prefer this method.

There are a number of reasons why a trader would want to go with position trading. These can include the following:

- Using the investment to help them in retirement
- Want to earn dividends each quarter as profit
- Less volatility in how much you will make
- You do not need to check the market every day
- You do not have to worry about short-term changes in the market
- The potential to make a lot of money as the company grows

Scalping

Scalping is another option you can work with. It is similar to day trading, but these trades often rely on just a few minutes to make a profit, rather than potentially a whole day.

The idea that comes with scalp trading is that you will make a ton of purchases of a stock and then sell it at a higher price as quickly as possible. You can only hold onto the stock for a day to make a scalp trading, but usually, you will not hold onto that security for more than five or 10 minutes. Sometimes you may be able to purchase a stock when it is on a discount on one of the markets, and then, turn around and sell it higher on a different market just a few minutes later to make a profit.

Any time that you see that there is a momentary down in the market, you are going to purchase the stock. Then, when the stock goes back up to average or above again, you will then sell that same stock. You will keep doing this a lot of these trades throughout the day, earning a small profit on each transaction that will add up to a good amount when you are done.

This works especially well if you see that a stock is selling for really low on one exchange, but there is a higher demand for it on another exchange. You can then purchase when it is low and sell it for a higher amount. You must be careful with this though because there are often fees and other things associated with it and you do not want to lose out on all your profits because of that.

This would also work within the same market though. You may find that there is a stock that seems to have a lot of ups and downs during the day. You can easily purchase the stock when it is at one of its lows so you get it at a good price. You would find these lows by watching the market and learning the trends for that share. Then, when the price goes back up, you would sell the stock again. This process could take just a few minutes to complete, or a few hours depending on the stock and the trends it follows.

Income Investing

The next option that you can go with is income investing. With this strategy, you want to take a look at companies with the idea that they will provide you with enough money to earn your living, or at least to provide you with a substantial flow of income. It is a simple idea. You just need to look for companies that are paying a high enough dividend that you could live off from that each year.

When you want to find a stock that will provide you with a steady stream of income, you will usually go with a safe option. This option will provide you with some return on investment, but will not have too much risk associated with it. This is why many people go with bonds and income securities, although you can do this with the stock market as well. You just need to find a company that can give you these returns for it to work.

Now, when working with income investing, you must pick a stock that provides its shareholders with a good dividend each quarter, or you will not be able to earn a good income. The average yield for many of the stocks will be three percent. But when you are trying to use this as an income source, you should aim to get six percent or more. This means the company you pick must pay a higher dividend payment than what you will see with others on the stock market or you will not make a good income.

In addition to being able to find a company who has a stock that will produce a steady and a predictable stream of income for you over many years, you should also look at the policies that are in place for the dividends. The income investor should consider whether one of the companies they want to invest inwill continue with the same dividend payment structure going into the future, or are thinking about changing it up.

If you decide to do this one and your research helps you find a company that was able to increase their dividends recently, then, this is something to look in to. You need to ask whether the company will be able to increase these dividends or if they are going to be able to remain steady in the future. If the company was able to do this for the past year straight, then, this is a good company to consider investing your money in.

The best way to ensure that this is going to work is to always do your research and see how a company did in the past. You can also look at some projections for the future as well. These will give you some outlook into whether the company will even pay dividends and if these dividends will be large enough for you to use as income.

Trading in Options

We talked about options a bit earlier. It is important to know how to trade with them if you decide that this is your choice for investing in the stock market. Options are going to be seen as a bit different than what you can do with the stock market. However, they are technically the same thing, so you can definitely do them here.

To keep it simple, an option is basically a derivative of a security. They are this way because the price that you are going to pay for that option is going to be linked to the price of something else. You are gaining a contract that is giving you the right to sell or buy the underlying asset at a predetermined price. You have the option to exercise this right or not though. However, you can only exercise this right either before or on the date that the option expires.

The right for you to purchase that option is known as a call option, and the right to sell that option is known as the put option. If you have heard about futures, you may recognize that there are some similarities here. They are however a bit different. For example, a future is going to make you have the rights and the obligations to purchase the security. With an option, you can choose to let the right pass without doing anything if the market does not work in your favor.

For example, if you would like to purchase some land in the next two years after some city regulations go through, you could purchase an option at $6,000 to provide an incentive for the seller to give it to you. If the regulations go through, the $6,000 will be the deposit towards the investment and you will be able to exercise the right to purchase the land at the price you and the seller agreed to. It does not matter what the market value of the land is at the time the city regulations passes, you will only need to pay what is in the option contract.

If the regulations do not go through and you decide not to purchase the land, you are not obligated to make the purchase. You will lose the $6,000 that you invested, but you do not need to purchase all that land if things do not work out.

This is an example of a commodity that you can purchase with options, but there are also a lot of stocks that you can purchase as options. Make sure to talk this over with your broker to see what stocks are available to do this way through them.

Chapter 13: How to Recognize That a Stock is a Bad Choice

While searching for the right stock in the market, you also need to be aware of some signs that a stock is not a good one to invest in. Some of the problems we are going to look at in this chapter show that a stock is not really doing that well and that it is a difficult investment. Some of the signs you should watch out for when trying to avoid a bad stock include:

The Debt-To-Equity Ratio is High

The first thing you need to check with a stock is whether the debt-to-equity ratio of the underlying business has started to increase. There are times when a business will start to rack up some extra debt. The reason it does this is the important part. If they gain more debt because they are acquiring a new patent or expanding, then it is not such a big deal. But if they have this debt because of an underperforming asset, a lawsuit, or excessive loans, it is a bad thing and you need to avoid this as much as possible.

Any business that has a high debt-to-equity ratio may not last long. They do not have enough leverage to work with so it is hard for the stock to maintain itself or manage. You should pick another stock to work with instead.

The Company's Cash Flow is Negative

There is always the chance that the stock you are looking at has a negative cash flow. When this happens, the cash flow that goes outward is going to be greater than the cash the business is earning. Sometimes, this could be because the business is using a lot of its money to expand. In some other cases, it shows that the company is unable to manage its assets in the proper manner.

Regardless of the reason, it is important to take this negative cash flow as a big warning sign that the stock may not be the best one to invest in. The best strategy is to inspect the stock to find out why the business has a negative cash flow to start with. This could be a sign of the business growing and they are just spending that money to thrive. If this is true, then, you can still consider that stock for purchase. But it could also be a big sign that the business is collapsing and you need to watch out for that.

Profit Warnings

As you are working with some of the news reading strategies, make sure that you learn to watch out for some of the profit warnings. This type of warning is a difficult report that is going to show how a company may not be doing as well as it had hoped. A company will release a report that basically says they are not going to meet their expectations, although they often hide it in other wordings and flowery prose. Make sure to keep a close eye on all your news readings to figure if there might be a price warning that you need to be aware of.

Insider Trading is Very Prominent

Insider trading is a serious problem, and it is also illegal. It is going to occur when people trade on a stock because they get insider information, which is supposed to be confidential. This illegal advantage can make the value of a stock change very quickly.

A company is supposed to report if some of its shares are bought by an insider, such as high-value shareholders or company directors. It has to explain who these insiders are, why they are investing in the stock, and how many shares they are going to buy. This ensures that people will have an idea why a stock is moving to a certain value. Insider trading can be a problem because those inside the company could pull off some trades to help make the value of a stock work in their favor without worrying about spending time on producing a report.

A High-Level Resignation Happens in the Company

The next issue that can tell you whether a stock is a bad one to go with is if there is a high-level resignation. When someone decides to resign from a position, there is a period of uncertainty in the market. If anything, it will show that a serious change could happen with that stock. This becomes a bigger problem if the person who resigns is not open about it. This could cause the value of the stock to go down.

Now, when someone resigns, it can have a negative impact on the stock. But if someone retires off the board, it is not going to really affect the stock. You should still watch it just in case, but the odds of the stock plummeting in value is not very likely. It often depends on how prominent that person was and how much influence they had over the whole company.

An Investigation by the SEC

An SEC investigation can occur at any time the business is believed to be doing something wrong. This can sometimes give off the impression that the stock is not doing any good because the business does not appear to be as strong as people think. A stock could be hurt by this type of investigation. These investigations are serious and you need to take precautions if you already own the stock because the value may be heading down.

Other Common Things to Watch with a Bad Stock

The following signs are ones that the stock is in trouble and you should not go with it. These are basic signs that might not show how a stock is going to lose money, but they may mean that the stock is going to have a harder time producing a profit for you. Some of the signs that you should watch out for include:

- A stock might be trading just above $10 a share for a long time, but it recently decreased to $10 or below.

- A stock ends up going through a big price decrease of 15 percent to 25 percent of its value in a short amount of time. You should definitely do some research to find out why this big drop happened.
- The value of the stock seems to reach a plateau and is not keeping up with the market at all.
- The earnings that come out for that stock are declining in value. Earnings consistently dropping every year can be a big problem for the company and for the investor. It is one thing to see the earnings decrease for a year, but it can be very concerning when this happens more often.
- The total volume of debt that is inside a particular company starts growing.
- The sales numbers and other financial factors end up looking small and meaningless when you compare them to how the competitor is doing.
- The P/E ratio is a lot higher than you would like to see in businesses of that same industry. It is even more concerning when you are not able to find a reason for why this ratio is going up in value rather than meeting the average for that industry.

With all of these signs that show how a stock is declining, you may have the assumption that you can just do a put order. In some cases, this will work.But in others, it is more about the stocks being in serious trouble, and a put order will not be able to save you. You have to be careful about investing in stocks with these signals because they can often guarantee that you are going to lose money on that trade.

Now, there is always a chance for a stock to rebound after just a few days, or even after a few weeks. The rebound sometimes occurs simply because the stock finally gets cheap enough that it shows as a discount and some people are excited to get in on it. This does not always happen so you need to always do your research and due diligence before you decide to trade or invest in a stock.

Chapter 14: Easy Tips to Help You Make the Most Money on the Stock Market

When you first get started in the stock market, there are a lot of things that you need to figure out. You have to come up with a savings amount so you can spend. You have to pick out a good platform to actually earn you money. And you need a solid stock and a good strategy to ensure that you can actually make money out of all this. This chapter is going to help make it easier for you by exploring some things you can do to get the most out of your stock market investment.

Find a Strategy That Works for You

As this guidebook went over, there are a lot of different strategies you can choose to try out to make money in the stock market. Some are really easy to use, while some are a bit more difficult. Some are going to work in a bullish market and others work better in a bearish market. There is a strategy that works well for everyone. You just need to find the right one for you.

Working in the stock market brings a lot of challenges, but one way to reduce these is by choosing a strategy and sticking with it. Too many investors start out with a strategy but find that it is not working for them or the market is turning in a different way than planned. They panic and quickly try to make some changes to save their investment.

Changing strategies right in the middle of a trade is a bad idea. It just would not work because each of them relies on different patterns to get the work done. If you start a trade and find that you are not that fond of it, it is fine for you to try out a new one. Just make sure that the particular trade has concluded before you move on to the new strategy.

As a beginner, you may try out a few different types of strategies to find the one that works best for you. But the important thing is to research them well and really know what you are looking into when you first get started. This ensures that you are able to give the strategy your full attention and effort before you move on.

Set Those Stop Points

We spent some time in this guidebook talking about the stop points and limit points to keep your losses down to a minimum. Some new investors figure they can watch the market on their own, and they do not take the time to actually work on these stop points and try to save themselves. These stop points are there to protect you in case you made a wrong prediction or in case the market goes completely wrong.

You can set a stopping point that is regular or trailing, or you can choose to go with an option for losing and for making profits. This ensures you earn as much as possible and limits your risks. You still need to spend some time researching and watching the market to ensure that the stock is performing the way that you want. But these stop points can certainly make it easier for a beginner and can save them some risk.

Leave Emotions out of the Game

Emotions are going to be your worst nightmare when you get started on the stock market. As soon as you let those emotions out, you will start to make some bad trades that will harm your ability to make money on the stock market. Once those emotions are set in place, your investment is going to be at risk. You will make poor decisions and leave your strategy in the dust.

For those who tend to give in to their emotions, it is best for you to find another form of investing. The stock market can be great, but it does have a lot of fluctuations and it is possible that you could lose all of your money if you are not careful.

Your emotions can lead you to stay in the stock market for too long. Sometimes we think that a trade will keep going up and we should stick with it to make enormous profits. But the market does level out over time and if you stay in too long, you may see the market turn on you and you will lose money.

It can go against you the other way too. If you see that you are losing money, then, get out and preserve your investment. Many new investors will stay in the market, even when they are losing, because they think they can get that money back if they just stay in for a little longer.

In either of these situations, you would have seen that the trend was going to reverse. The charts we have been talking about this whole guidebook can help you notice when a trend is about to occur, and you can make the appropriate changes and work to get in and out of the trades at the right time. Sometimes this will save you from losing too much money in the process, and other times it will help you earn money.

Try out Some Platforms Before Deciding

You should take some time trying out a few platforms before you decide which one is the best for your needs. Some platforms are just easier to work with, while some may have lag times that could make you lose money. Some will just have more features than others. Each trader is going to find that different aspects are important to them, and knowing which aspects are the most important for you can help you pick out a platform.

Often, you get a trial run on these platforms before you decide to use them. If you get this option, take your time. You want to explore the platform. Maybe do a practice run with a trade, and be very thorough. You are going to use this platform to help you make money in the stock market. Because of this, you want to make sure that the platform works properly and has everything you need to make trading as easy as possible.

Learn the fees That Each Broker Charges

Each broker is going to charge a different fee for working with them. Some are going to focus their fees on each individual trade. Others are going to charge a commission from what you earn. The one that you go with can sometimes depend on the type of trading you want to work with.

For example, if you plan to do just a few long-term trades and enjoy earning dividends on those companies for a long time to come, then, going with a flat rate per trade is probably going to be the best. If you are not trading that much, then, these flat fees are not going to cut into your profits that much.

If you choose to go with something like day trading, you may want to lean more toward the commissions. The commission ensures that you only pay a little bit out of pocket, rather than having to pay each time you do a trade. Day trading can involve a lot of little trades over the course of the day. Each trade may only net you a little bit of money, but if you are able to do that a bunch of times, you will earn a higher profit. But if you are paying $5 per trade, you will have a hard time keeping up with day trading.

Find a Mentor

The next thing that you can try to do is to find a mentor to work with. There are many people who have spent time in the stock market and have learned the right tips and tricks to make the most out of their money with the fewest dollars out of their pocket. If you can find someone who is willing to work with you and show you the ropes, you are going to be way ahead of everyone else who just got started in the stock market.

This does not mean that you should just blindly follow what your mentor tells you. With the stock market, you need to follow your own gut and intuition and listen to the risks that you are willing to take and nothing else. Your mentor is sure to give you a lot of advice. Some of the advice will be good, but you need to pay attention to what you feel comfortable doing and make some of your own decisions. The money you spend in the stock market is yours, so treat it as such and you will make some great trades.

Try Working with Dogs of the Dow While You Get Used to the Market

One easy strategy to use when you first start in the stock market is the Dogs of the Dow. Each year, a new list of the best-performing stocks on the market is released. You would simply look at this list and invest in the top 10. This allows you to have time to diversify your portfolio quite a bit. Most stocks on this list are doing well and are secure, so you get the added bonus of having dividend payments without having to look hard at charts and figure.

When the year ends, you go through and check the list again. There are times when you may have to change the stocks you are trading because they are no longer in the top 10 of this list. It is an easy way for a beginner to diversify their portfolio, make some money, and get some time to learn about the market before jumping in.

This does not mean that you can just purchase the stocks and not look at them for a year. This strategy is a great one for beginners because it is often better than what other strategies have. There are still times when a stock on this list will fall or run into trouble. Even if you go with this option, make sure to take it slowly and watch the stocks to make sure you keep earning money on your investments.

If You Do a Bad Trade, Consider Taking a Break

There are times when one of your trades is going to be less than stellar. You may have read the charts the wrong way, jumped into a trade too quickly, or just made overall bad trading decisions in the hopes of making a lot of money quickly. If you go through a particularly bad trade, it may be best for you to take a few days off from trading.

Many new traders run into problems when they have a bad trade and do not take off a few days. They get emotionally involved. They feel bad about losing that money, and they want to be able to earn it back as quickly as possible. They often get caught up in revenge trading, where they will try to take bigger and bigger risks in the hopes of earning that money back. But since they are only focused on making money back quickly, they are going to make really bad decisions that will cause them to lose even more money.

The break does not have to be a long one. A week is plenty of time for most people. It, however, gives you the chance to take a step back, look at your trading strategy, and see if you need to make changes without emotions associated with the loss getting in the way.

Getting started on the stock market can be a great experience. You have the potential to make a lot of money in a short amount of time, or even over the long-term, as long as you make good and sound decisions. Follow some of the tips in this chapter, and you will be trading in the stock market like a professional in no time.

Conclusion

Thank for making it through to the end of *Stock Market Investing for Beginners*. Let us hope it was informative and was able to provide you with all the tools you need to achieve your goals.

The next step is to decide how you want to get into the market. There are a lot of choices when it comes to how you would like to invest your money, but the stock market offers the most diversity out of all of them. You can choose which company you want to invest in, how long you want to stay in the market, and how much you want to invest.

This guidebook took some time to look over all the options that you have when it comes to investing in the stock market. We looked at the basics of the stock market, some of the different types of securities that you can choose, and the best strategies that will help you make a profit each time you do a trade. We even spent time talking about trading the margin, how to know when a stock is a good one or not, and the best tips to get the most out of trading even when you are just starting.

When you are ready to get started with your investment in the stock market, make sure to check this guidebook to help you make a profit and put your money to work for you.

Finally, if you found this book useful in anyway, a review on Amazon is always appreciated!

Investing

Introduction

Investing is a way of saving money that scares a lot of people, because if we are being honest, it is scary! You are taking a chance on something to either make you a lot of money or perhaps lose your initial investment. That is something that other investment books tend to gloss over, but we want you to be mentally prepared for the emotional roller-coaster that can be the stock market. This isn't to say that you cannot make money or that it is impossible for the everyday person to be able to make money by investing wisely. But "wisely" is the key phrase here.

In this book we are going to show you not only where and how to invest your hard-earned money, but we are also going to break down the language barrier that exists between stock market experts and everyone else. By the time you are done, you are going to be able to invest your money with confidence and see that when you invest wisely, it's not so much of a gamble.

But first we would like to talk to you about why you are going to want to invest, period. Investing is the best way to make your money work for you. Sure, you could continue to put money away in a bank savings account that nets you maybe half a percent of interest per year, but that is barely better than just stuffing the money in your mattress. Investing puts your money to work through compound interest. We are going to explain that concept a little further later on in this book, but for now, realize that compound interest is the way to make sure you're making money even when you're asleep.

So many Americans are not saving for retirement. Too many. It is a sad reality that by the time these folks are ready to say goodbye to their nine-to-five, they will have nothing saved up to sustain them throughout their retirement years. The good news for you is that you are reading this book, which means that you do not want to find yourself with tumbleweeds in your bank account when you're ready to retire. We are going to introduce you to the world of investing by not only giving you the how-to's of investing, but also arming you with knowledge about the terminology and who to trust. If you follow our methods and invest wisely, you can turn yourself into a millionaire by the time you retire.

We are also going to include a list of must-read books and must-watch documentaries and films for you to enjoy. We included these sources because we think that if you read and watch, you will gain even more investment knowledge that you can put to good use. We also have some profiles on people who have gone from literal rags to riches through using their money wisely and exhibiting the characteristics that we think are important in making a good investor.

Chapter 1: Why Investing is Important

You might be wondering to yourself why you would bother risking your money by investing it when you could just park it in a bank account and add to it throughout the years. Yes, this will certainly be a safe way to save up money, but over time, you will actually lose money due to inflation. If you are able to invest and you invest wisely, you can earn money with money – a strange concept, we know, but stick with us here.

Let's say you just keep socking away money in your savings account, adding in $300 every paycheck. Assuming you have around 30 years to retirement and you get paid twice per month, you are looking at $216,000. Now, that's nothing to sneeze at, but that is also not going to last you very long in retirement. You need to think about things like the possibility of high medical bills, perhaps having to go live in a nursing home, and many other life factors that come into play when you get older.

However, let's say you take that $300 per paycheck and you put it in investments that earn you six percent a year and compounds quarterly. At the end of thirty years, you will have made yourself $605, 263.53! Now, that is still not enough to retire safely on, but if you consider that it is just one of your investments, the possibility of retiring as a millionaire becomes ever closer.

So let us explore exactly what compound interest is. It's so fantastic we just have to tell you all we can about it. Compound interest is what is known in the industry as interest that calculates upon interest. It is what makes investors so successful and continually funds their retirement accounts and also pads their bank accounts while they are still working. Here is a breakdown of how it works in the real world. Let us say that you take that $1000 you get for your birthday and you put it in an account that yields one percent in interest per year. That interest is calculated on that initial $1000. The same thing happens next year – one percent of that $1000 is added. And so on. So you are making money, but at a snail's pace. Nobody is going to get rich from that.

Instead, let us say that you take that same $1000 and invest it in a fund where you get compound interest. For argument's sake, we will give you a six percent return. That first year, you will get six percent of that $1000 added to your balance, for a new total of $1060. So far, not different from that boring old savings account. But it is the second year of investing where things heat up. Now your interest is calculating on that $1060, not the original principal of $1000. So the second year of your investment you recoup $63.60, bringing your total up to $1,123.60. Not bad right? The best part is, with compound interest, your money is working for you even while you sleep.

So how will you be a millionaire by retirement? Compound interest. Shop around and see if you can find an account that will get you at least 8%. Next, see how often your interest compounds – the more often the better.

Here is the tough part, though: you cannot just put a lump sum in the account and then forget about it. Yes, it is one way to earn money, but we are not trying to get you to be an average investor with this book – we are trying to teach you how to be a millionaire by the time you are ready to retire. Because who doesn't want to be able to retire and not worry about money? Just sit back, sip rum out of a coconut and spend time with the grandkids.

So, like I said, here's the tough part. You have to consistently add to your investment. You have to consistently put money aside into your investment accounts so that the money can keep building. The more money you add, the more money there is for the interest to calculate on and then the more money you end up with by the time you're ready to sail off into the sunset.

And here's the really, really tough part: do not touch that money! Don't touch it to get that new car you've been wanting, don't touch it to buy your wife that new diamond ring, don't touch it to buy that new house you really don't need. This is not an emergency fund to bail you out – this is literally going to be the difference between life and death for you once you quit your job once and for all. Not to mention that this is going to be a way for you to maybe even quit that job a little earlier than you intended.

A Word About Rainy Day Funds

So I know we just rained on your parade (see what we did there) about rainy day funds and about how you'd be losing money to inflation. That is all true, but it is still important to have at least six months worth of salary saved up. Because life happens. You get an unexpected hospital bill, your cat needs to go to the emergency room, or maybe your kid just needs braces. It helps to be prepared for when these things happen – so take a little bit of your paycheck and start building a rainy day fund.

The really cool thing about living in this digital age is that there are so many options available to investors who are just willing to put in a little time and effort. This means that even for your rainy day fund, you can find so many automated ways to save that sometimes even offer interest! For example, something that has become very popular among Millennials is the Digit app. It is a handy little app that you hook up to your bank account. It reads your spending habits and will automatically save money for you. It even pays interest and pays you for referrals. It's worth looking into and will help you save up for that rainy day in no time.

In our next chapter, we will take a look at the stock market and introduce you to some basic fundamentals.

Chapter 2: Some Stock Market Fundamentals

In this chapter, we are going to take you through the basics of the stock market – stocks, bonds, what the stock market is exactly, and why investing in the stock market always means that you are going to take a risk.

What are stocks?

Stocks are one of many tools in the investor's tool belt that helps them build up wealth. Stocks are, basically speaking, shares of a company that you can buy, sell, and trade. Imagine that the company is made up of millions of bricks – if you own one of the bricks, you own part of the company. More officially, stocks are what is known in the industry as a security – one that signals to other investors that you own part of Company X.

But stock is not just stock – there are two types. One is called common and the other is preferred. Common stock is stock that entitles its owners to vote at board meetings (usually through a proxy) and they also share in dividends that are paid. The other type, preferred, has other benefits, though they do not include having a vote at board meetings. The benefit of having preferred stock is if the company should go bankrupt, you will get paid ahead of those who just have common stock.

While stock is merely one tool in the tool belt, it is perhaps one of the most popular and also the one that will yield the highest results over the long term. If you are investing in stock, it is important to remember that this is going to be for the long term. If you want to be able to pull your money out in less than five years, you will have better luck parking your money in a CD (which we will explain further later in this book) or just putting it in a savings account. Stocks are meant to be held for a minimum of five to ten years. So just be aware that when you are making this particular investment, you are foregoing that money for several years. But it is all for a good cause.

What are bonds?

Remember taking out those student loans in undergrad? Remember understanding that you were getting money, the loan company was getting a note promising that you would repay them after a certain time passed after graduation? Well, that was probably your first experience with bonds; aside from those savings bonds your grandma got you for your christening.

Bonds are when a company borrows money from you and then promises to repay you at a certain time and with interest. A bond is an essential way for a company to finance itself. Companies use bonds to pay for new projects, research and development, and marketing. Most bonds are sold at a fixed rate of interest. This means that no matter what happens in the stock market during the time you hold the bond, the company is responsible for paying you five percent a year in interest.

But, the interesting part is that while the interest rate will stay the same over the life of the bond, that interest rate may make it a better or worse investment at any time during the life of the bond. For example, if other bonds with the same face value were paying three percent, then you would be getting a great deal at five percent. But if others were paying seven percent, you might be a little bit unhappy because the price of the bond goes down, putting itself at a discount until its effective rate is five percent. Basically, when interest rates go up, bond prices go down. Inversely, when interest rates go down, bond prices go up.

Bonds tend to have similar traits, despite being sold for different purposes and for different companies:

- All bonds have a face value. A bond's face value is what it will be worth at the end of its life. It is also what the interest is calculated on during its life. So if you buy Bond X for $1000 while interest rates are up and someone else buys that same bond for $1050 while interest rates are down, both of you will get the same face value of $1000 once the bond matures.
- All bonds have a coupon rate. The coupon rate is a fancy way of saying it is the interest rate on the bond. So if the coupon rate on your Bond X is 7%, then you get $1000 x 7%, or $70 each year while you hold the bond.
- All bonds have coupon dates. These are dates when the interest on the bond will be paid. Coupon dates vary, but they usually are once or twice a year.

- All bonds have a maturity date. This is the date upon which you will receive the face value of the bond.
- All bonds have an issue price. Think of this as the sticker price for buying the bond. This is different than its face value, which is what you will get at the end of the bond's life.

You are going to want to pick your bonds carefully, just like any investment. Bonds are not as volatile as stocks, but they still are always a risk. So, you are going to want to pick bonds from issuers who have a good credit rating. It's the same principal that people use when deciding to lend you money. If you have a good credit rating, it increases the odds that you will pay back the money that is lent to you because you have a good history of repaying your debts. If you have a poor credit score, or a poor credit history, it signals to lenders that you are not good with your money and so are more likely to default on your loan.

Categories of Bonds

Bonds have three different categories in which they can fall:
- Corporate bonds – these are issued bycorporations
- Municipal bonds – these are government bonds. What's fun about these is that sometimes their coupon payments (interest payments) can be treated as tax-free income by the issuing municipality.
- U.S. Treasury bonds, notes, and bills – the difference between these three is the maturity dates. Bonds are usually held for longer than ten years, notes between one and ten years, and bills are usually held for less than 12 months.

Bond Varieties

- **<u>Zero coupon bonds:</u>** here, you do not get your regular interest payments. The bond instead is issued to you at a discount (less than face value) and then once it matures, you get the face value.
- **<u>Convertible bonds:</u>** these are a little bit more complicated and maybe a little too complicated for the first-time investor. But, for your edification, these are bonds that eventually can be converted

into equity. This will really only happen if it makes sense price-wise to make that change. Remember, bonds are not equity.

- **<u>Callable bonds:</u>** again, this is a little complicated for the beginner investor, but these are something to look out for as you gain experience in the stock market. These types of bonds are able to be recalled by the company that issued them if the interest rates drop to a certain point.

So what's the difference?

First, stocks are actual shares in a company. They give you certain rights and their values will fluctuate much more than the value of bonds. Bonds are not equity. They do not give you a stake in a company; rather, they are shares of debt. Bonds also are not as volatile as stocks and will guarantee you a payout at the end of their maturity, all things being equal and the company does not become insolvent.

What exactly is the stock market?

I remember sitting in my very first economics class in undergrad and feeling like my brain was going to explode when my teacher tried to explain the concept of the stock market. I felt like this whole thing was a sham and how could we possibly trust actual cash money to this ridiculous thing? But then the more I thought about it, the more I realized that it made as much sense as using a credit card, or taking out those student loans that were paying for my seat. I promise you, if you give us a chance, we can help you understand the stock market and see that it really isn't as complicated as it seems.

So the first thing you need to understand is the power of supply and demand. Imagine it like this: imagine you are the person who first discovered coffee. (How amazing would that be, right? You could put Starbucks to shame if your ancestors were the ones who discovered coffee.) Anyway, so you've discovered the magical bean that now everyone and their mother needs to properly function in the morning. You have created demand. They want it, you've got it. And assuming that you're the only one who has it, you can charge whatever price you like. This is because supply is limited. You're only one person after all and there is only so much coffee you can harvest in a day by yourself. But imagine that someone else discovers that they, too, can grow coffee. Suddenly, another coffee-seller has entered the market. Now there is an additional supply chain for coffee. If demand stays the same, then you are going to see a drop in your prices. This is because there is greater supply now to keep up with the demand. And that is the beast of supply and demand. We can try to blame high prices on as many things as we can, but even if we account for every other variable, if there is greater demand and less supply, prices will skyrocket. Inversely, if there is a greater supply and demand stays the same or decreases, then prices will take a nosedive.

Supply and demand really is the driver behind the stock market. It is the principle that drives life itself, really. But this isn't a philosophy book, it's a book on investments.

The stock market is actually a made up of many different exchanges and markets where everything from stocks, bonds, and other types of securities are traded. Basically, it's where companies go when they need funding. They trade pieces of themselves for your money so they can do things like produce your laptop and fund whatever it is that Elon Musk is up to these days. Of course, these pieces of a company do not have the same value every single day or even every single hour.

So what does this mean for investors? Well, fluctuation means risk. Let's say you buy $500 worth of stock on Tuesday. Things look really good for a week and you see that the company you invested in is about to launch a new product that looks promising. That new promising product makes the company seem more valuable and all of a sudden your $500 investment is now worth $1000! What a great day, right? That means you should go out and put that down payment on your new house and buy a bottle of bubbly, right?

Nope. Because in this scenario, let's say that the product launch flops, the CEO is hauled away in handcuffs, and the company has gone bankrupt. Now you are left with absolutely nothing, not even your $500, if you owned common stock. You're also on the hook for that down payment and you probably spent way too much money on that bottle of champagne.

This is almost exactly what happened during the stock market crash in 2008. We all know what a disaster that was. Basically, people who had no business getting approved to $100,000 homes were getting approved for mortgages at ridiculously low rates. These people who were often living either at or just above the poverty line were on the hook for the $100,000 mortgages. Those mortgages were then bundled together and sold as securities to fund other ventures for companies. Eventually, when those people defaulted on their mortgages, and did so en masse, all of those security bundles became worthless. People lost billions of dollars. Except for a few people who ended up shorting the market, but we will talk about those guys later in the book. It's an interesting story, so make sure you keep reading for that.

Measures of Performance

We need to talk for a moment about how we can see how the stock market is doing. You are going to want to keep an eye on the stock indexes. They are tools that people use to take note of the changes in the values of the different exchanges in the stock market.

Many different indexes and exchanges make up the stock market and they often touch and overlap. Several examples of indexes are the NASDAQ Composite Index, the Standard and Poor (S & P) 500 and of course, the Dow Jones Industrial Average.

The S & P 500 and the Dow Jones Industrial Average are the two most popular indexes for measuring stock performance. As the name indicates, the Standard and Poor 500 are made up of the 500 biggest companies in the United States in terms of capitalized stocks traded. The Dow Jones Industrial Average is made up of the 30 largest companies in the United States, and those stocks' price affects the average. So when stock prices soar, the Dow also soars.

So when you see people freaking out about the Dow and the S & P, it is because those two indexes are really good indicators for how the market is doing overall. So while you may not have stock that is actually in either index, it is likely that your stock's price will be affected by the performance of these two indexes.

How do these indexes affect me?

So, we have talked about how the stock market is a convergence of markets and exchanges from all over the world. This means that stocks and bonds are subject to the butterfly effect. So if something overseas were to affect a company here in America, then the stock price would reflect that. Let's give a more concrete example: if there was panic in Japan about the costs of Japanese steel, then we might see over here a sudden increase price of American steel because the demand has gone up. Demand hasn't increased here, but it has increased elsewhere and we all know that supply and demand rule the world.

We see, though, how these indexes affect our daily lives. When we see that the Dow and S & P are doing well, things overall seem to be hunky-dory. Gas prices remain steady, sales taxes stay down, prices for everyday goods remain the same or even go down. But God forbid those indexes do poorly – you would think sometimes that it's the zombie apocalypse about to devour us all. Gas prices go up, your kids' notebooks that you buy at Walmart are suddenly much more expensive than you remember.

So this principle will extend to your investments as well. Even if you don't have a stake in either index, your investments will be affected. This is because all of the stocks and bonds that are traded on the public markets deal with funds that are traded on those bigger indexes. So they are all interdependent. When one has a good day, we all have a good day. So pay attention to the stock market when you begin to invest – keep an eye on the Dow and the Standard and Poor indexes. It will give you an idea on what to expect for your investments both that day and for a little bit into the future.

But please, remember that unless you have sunk all of your money into Elon Musk's newest outlandish venture like a Mars colony, it is no reason to lose your mind if the Dow loses a few points. Your everyday life will still probably be fine, aside from those other things we talked about. So don't yell at your kids or kick the dog when the Dow loses a few points – just keep your cool and remember that investing in the stock market is a rollercoaster that you willingly signed up for.

So what does this mean for me at the end of the day?

The moral of the story here is that you should not be investing more than you can comfortably lose. This is also why you should be keeping that rainy day fund nice and padded – you never know what is going to come around the bend in the stock market. It could be a bear or a bull – you need to be ready for either.

In our next chapter, we are going to discuss the different types of investment tools that are available to you outside of stocks and bonds. Keep in mind that these aren't every single possible kind of investment, but these will give you a great start. Read on!

Chapter 3: Different Types of Investment Tools

CDs

No, these aren't pieces of what now is outdated technology that used to have songs on them. CDs are certificates of deposit. It's a savings account that has a date when it becomes mature and an interest rate that is fixed from the date you open the account. It is a good tool for folks who maybe have a hard time with that "don't touch" part of the whole saving thing. See, you can't really touch the money that is in that account.

Typically, a CD works by you putting a certain amount of money into a specific account with a financial institution that has a desirable rate of interest. You let that money grow for the specified amount of time and then at the end of the life of the certificate of deposit, you get your initial investment plus interest. These investments are good for people who are looking to have competitive rates of interest without the volatility of the stock market. Also, they are insured for up to $250,000 by the FDIC, which means that even if the bank goes belly-up, you will get at least the money you invested back. Also, you need to remember that if you withdraw your money early, you will face financial penalties. Again, this helps people keep their hands out of the proverbial cookie jar.

Some common CDs with good interest rates can be found at Pentagon Federal Credit Union, First Internet Bank of Indiana, and M.Y. Safra Bank, FSB. Each of these institutions requires a minimum deposit of $1000 and will pay 3.30% in interest each year. These are incredibly competitive rates and again, are federally insured.

Mutual Funds

I will confess, I love a good mutual fund. They are a great investment tool for first time investors. This is because you pick your fund, you deposit your money to get things started, and someone else handles the distribution of risk and your asset allocation. That is a fancy way of saying that an expert will help determine your mix of investment securities and how much risk you are exposed to. So this is part of my love-letter to mutual funds.

Mutual funds are a stack of bonds and stocks that are invested in a multitude of different companies that make different things and have different risks. What makes mutual funds different than an individual portfolio is that mutual funds bring together investors from all around the world, pool their money, and then buy a mix of stocks and bonds that they deem worthy. Think of it like this: you and a bunch of friends get together and decide that you want to start investing. You hire an expert to tell you where to invest your money and how much. This expert puts together a portfolio for you all. Each of you puts up a different amount of money, based on what you can afford.

This means that each of you owns a different percentage of the mutual fund and will receive your payments accordingly. So someone who has put five thousand dollars into the fund will of course receive greater dividends than someone who has invested one thousand. But you will all be invested in the same stocks and bonds, just in different amounts. So how do you earn money? Well, same as you would on a regular investment. You will earn dividends on your stocks and if you sell a security that has gone up in price, then you will earn a profit. And finally, let's say that those same securities increase in price but you don't sell the individual securities. You can just sell off portions of your mutual fund. You can then reap the profits from that.

The top three mutual funds for your retirement are Vanguard Institutional Index I, American Funds Euro Pacific Growth F1, and Fidelity Freedom 2030. Vanguard, over a ten-year period, will earn you 7.5%. Over that same time period, American Funds will earn you 3.0% and Fidelity will earn you 4.4%. These are all incredibly competitive rates of return and are worth examining further.

Annuities

Annuities are a way for you to have a steady stream of income from a single investment. Sounds pretty good, right? Basically, you invest a sum of money, you let it grow, and then at a set time in the period, you start getting regular payments from that investment. The idea here is that this will help you in your later years so that you do not outlive your retirement.

As you might imagine, there are different kinds of annuities. There are fixed and variable annuities, with different subcategories therein.

A fixed annuity means that on your investment, you will earn a steady stream of interest. This means that you will get the same amount of money each year. These are the kinds of annuities you will want to focus on if you are risk-averse because they do not depend on the stock market.

Within the overarching category of fixed annuities are immediate annuities and deferred annuities. Fixed annuities are investment products where you invest a single lump sum. Then, within a very short time you start receiving your payments. Typically you want this kind of annuity if you are close to retiring. The other type of fixed annuity is the deferred annuity. This is when you don't need the money soon, and are able to put off receiving your payments for a few years. The problem with this kind of annuity is that you will have to pay taxes on whatever payouts you receive.

But, unlike mutual funds, you can withdraw a certain amount of money early from these funds without incurring a tax penalty, which is useful, because like we have said many times before: life just happens sometimes. The estate tax also does not apply to annuities, which is another bonus if you want to leave your annuity to a loved one in your will. The biggest bonus about these funds is that you have thirty days to completely withdraw from the annuity contract before you are committed. This is incredibly useful for those investors who perhaps are new to the game and need to change their minds before committing to a fund.

Variable annuities take either a lump sum or several payments. The issuer will make consistent payments to you right then and there or at some point in the future. What is so interesting about these funds is that it's like you took a stock portfolio (or a mutual fund), your life insurance, and your retirement plan and combined them all together to make a super-investment. You are free to select from various mutual funds when you sign up for a variable annuity. The choices are endless!

A variable annuity breaks down into two time-periods as outlined below:

1. The accumulation time period: this is when you are paying into the investment. You can pick and choose your investment options – stocks, bonds, mutual funds, etc. Depending on how your portfolio does, you will either make or lose money. Before investing, you are going to want to make sure you do your research to see the fund's performance over time, how much it

pays in interest and dividends, and how much risk it exposes itself to.

2. The payout time period: this seems self-explanatory, but during this time-period, you reap the benefits of your investments. You can either take payments over time or you can get a single lump-sum payment. These payments, just like with other annuities, are guaranteed by the issuing agency.

   a. A quick note on the lump-sum payments: generally speaking, you are always going to want to go with the annuity payments versus the lump-sum. I always cringe when I see lottery winners take the lump sum versus the annuity payments. Not only are you going to be stuck paying the taxes on that entire lump sum, but you risk losing it all because you spend it. Better take the annuity option and ensure that you get a check every year.

Stock Portfolios

A stock portfolio is the slimmed down version of the mutual fund. Instead of exposing yourself to a mix of different types of investment securities, you just buy different stocks in different markets and with different levels of risk.

Building on that concept, investors have come up with a "bucket" approach for stock portfolios. You have two buckets – the risky and the safe. For the risky bucket, you are going to want to maximize your return for your risk. This means you are going to want to design a global equity portfolio. This is the kind of portfolio that gives you a taste of all of the securities that are traded around the world. The safe bucket will include things like treasury bonds and certificates of deposit. Their return will not be particularly high, but they will at least expose you to less risk than your other bucket. Here, you would be looking at similar rates of return, as you would see on the certificates of deposits that we mentioned above.

Day Trading

As a beginner in the investment world, you will probably not be ready to quit your nine-to-five job and become a day trader. A day trader is exactly that – they sit in front of their computers, usually with more than one monitor, and they watch the markets all day and monitor their investments. They have to be ready and willing at a moment's notice to make a trade that is to their benefit. And here's the thing: they aren't always right! Unless you have years of experience with the stock market, there is absolutely no guarantee that you will even be able to make a dime by day trading.

Even if you are the most successful hedge fund manager in the world, you still may run into problems. There is a reason why we keep mentioning in this book that investing is a gamble – that's because it is! Every time a day trader presses a button on their dashboard to buy or sell, they are taking a risk. And they need to be able to live with that risk. If you get nervous just waiting in line for your Starbucks, it is highly unlikely that you will be able to make it as a day trader.

But let's say you decide that you want to just jump off the cliff and start diving. Well, you're going to need to find an online platform that is going to allow you to have instant access and up to date information on the various markets. The most common example would be E*Trade. With this trading platform, you pay a certain cost per trade and depending on your particular package, you may not pay any fees for trades at all.

A quick aside about fees, by the way. You need to watch out for them. Later on in this book we are going to talk about brokers and how you can pick ones that you can trust. It is going to be important for you to realize that even fees as "low" as one percent can erode literally thousands of dollars from your investments over the years. The idea here is not to be losing money unnecessarily, right? So why would you pay fees that high? Pay attention to whatever you sign, electronically or in person, because there are hidden fees literally everywhere. So, aside over – just do your homework.

Anyway, back to E*Trade. So, you will need about $500 to put into the most basic account. After your account is fully funded, you can log onto your dashboard and start trading. Once you have decided on your particular fund makeup, you can watch its performance and buy, sell, and trade as necessary. But again, this is really more for the advanced investor. You will get there, but we would recommend that you experiment with the other tools in this book before you jump off that particular cliff.

Speaking of jumping off a cliff, it's getting time for you to think about making the decision to make the leap into the investment world. In the next chapter, we will discuss how you can get started on investing now.

Chapter 4: How to Get Started Now

By now, I am sure that you are done theorizing and are ready to get started on actually investing. So this chapter is going to be devoted to walking you through how to buy stocks. We will walk you through the in-person (gasp!) and the online portion of how to buy stocks.

How to buy stocks online

Honestly, in this digital age, it is so much easier to just buy your investments online. You don't need to put on real pants or brush your hair, and you can still make tons of money. So, first, you are going to need to pick an online platform. There are literally thousands of them, but if you are looking to buy and trade stocks online, you are going to want to go through either AmeriTrade or E*Trade.

We have talked about E*Trade before, so we will continue to use them in our example. You are going to have to input all of your information into their online platform, sign all the disclosures, and then fund your account. You will pick your stocks and tell your online broker which ones and how many of each to purchase. Typically you will pay a fee per trade, but again, you can avoid these fees if you go with different packages or if you end up making more than a certain number of trades per month. Again, do your homework.

So once you decide on your particular mix of stocks, you execute your trades. You either pick a market order or a limit order. The difference is that when you execute a market order, you are buying the stock at whatever the market price is at that particular moment. A limit order is when you have your online broker set to pounce on a stock when it hits a certain price.

You don't have to depend on one of these online platforms, though – you can also buy the stocks directly from the company through sites like DRIPInvestor.com. However, if you do this, you won't have the same freedom to buy and sell all the different types of stocks that you would like to have in your particular portfolio.

How to Buy Funds

You buy mutual funds in a similar way in which you buy your stocks. You are going to want to pick a fund that has the right type of investment and risk allocation for you. This might mean that you have a risk allocation of just a few hundred dollars in highly volatile stocks and then the rest in safe investments like CDs or treasury bonds. And of course the inverse would be true if you are a particularly risky investor.

You can go through big companies like Vanguard, T. Rowe Price, or Fidelity. You can also go to a rather big exchange and buy a fund that has pieces from funds at those big mutual fund companies. Simply go online, set up your account, and get started.

There are so many different kinds of funds to choose from, but we will list a few here just to get you started:

- **Index funds**: these are funds that are going to reflect whatever index they are a part of. So, you could get a fund that is tied to the Dow or to the Standard and Poor 500. These are easy to keep an eye on because as long as you are paying attention to those particular indexes, you will get to see how your funds are doing.
- **Actively-managed funds**: as you can probably guess, these are funds that are going to be managed by a broker. The handy part here is that the broker is going to be the one to pick the individual stocks and bonds and decide on the allocation of risk throughout the portfolio. So you are paying someone to do all of the research and worrying for you. Of course, this also means that you are going to have less control and also will be paying higher fees. But for someone who is brand new to investing, this might be worth it in the beginning. After all, once you learn some more about the stock market, you can pull out and manage your fund yourself.

- **Lifecycle funds/target date funds**: these are funds that combine stocks and bonds into a portfolio. So basically you are taking a piece of different mutual funds and sticking them together rather like a Picasso. And like a Picasso, they can really end up being quite valuable at the end of the day. Again, this is the type of fund where you are having other people pick the funds that you are investing in. This is useful for the beginner who doesn't really have a clue about which fund to pick and wants to get a head start on the game. The allocation of funds will change as you inch closer to leaving your nine-to-five for good.

- **Lifestyle funds**: these are just like the funds mentioned just above, but their risk allocation does not change over time. It stays the same. The key here is that sometimes in these funds, there are extra fees. Remember how we feel about fees? We don't like them. They steal money from your pocket that you could eventually use in the future.

- **Balanced funds:** these are fairly self-explanatory. You are going to have a risk-averse blend of stocks and bonds. This means that you will have about 40% of your money in bonds and the remaining 60% in stocks.

- **Tax managed funds**: these types of funds are useful for those of us who are trying to avoid paying taxes that are unnecessary. Without getting into a whole philosophical debate about paying taxes, suffice it to say that this will help you keep the taxes you will have to pay on what you earn from these funds to an absolute minimum.

How to Buy Tracker Funds

A tracker fund is a fund that going to cover a broad market segment or exchange. It is very similar to an index fund. Remember those? Index funds are asset mixes whose performance is tied to the index that it tracks. So, if you have a Dow index fund and the Dow does well on Thursday, then you are going to have a good Thursday. These types of funds are helpful for those investors who want to have a broad exposure to different funds at a relatively low initial cost.

Again, you can buy these online. The most popular tracker fund is the SPDR S&P 500 ETF (SPY). This tracker fund has $249.2 billion in assets, an annual volume of 62.04 million shares, and a year to date return of 16.31%. That's pretty amazing for a first time investor.

So Where Can I Go?

TD Ameritrade, Fidelity, Vanguard, and E*Trade are all excellent places to go online and begin to invest. They are easy to use, relatively low-cost, and provide excellent customer support. These are all vital aspects of a trading platform for any investor, let alone one that is just starting out.

If you wanted a brick and mortar institution, Charles Schwab, Edward Jones, and Merrill Lynch are excellent institutions to go to. They are all trusted investment companies that have stood the test of time. They are also highly regulated by the SEC, which means that the government watches them like a hawk. The government watches every move they make and heavy penalties are imposed even if there is just a hint of wrongdoing. So if you wanted to go in and talk to a broker, you would be in good hands there.

That being said, remember that brokers are going to charge you fees. These fees can end up costs you thousands upon thousands of dollars over the years that you are investing. Certainly fees have decreased industry-wide, but if you are a first-time investor, sometimes those fees can be a high barrier to entry. Also, it is worth noting that some of these institutions, Merrill Lynch in particular, will not assign you an individual broker unless you are worth at least $250,000. I don't know about you, but when I first began investing, I was not worth a quarter of a million dollars. I was trying to get to that point.

At the end of the day, I would recommend sticking with the online brokers for now. As you build up your net worth and gain more experience, maybe you can move into one of the big brokerage houses. For now, though, take it easy, save yourself some money, and invest online.

Okay, But When Do I Sell?

First, you need to remember that the decision to buy and sell is not one that should be taken lightly or made hastily. You do not need to sell your stocks at the first sign of trouble and you should not buy investments just because the market is in a lull. There are several things you need to consider when making the decision to buy and sell. You are going to want to buy into an investment, first and foremost, when you have done all of your research and determined that it is an investment that matches the amount of risk you are comfortable with and also matches the amount of money you can put towards it at that very moment. If it's a stock, buy it when it is stable and there is nothing volatile going on in the market. If it is a bond, buy it when it is at a discount. That way you will end up making money when it matures. If you buy at $1000 bond at a discount for $950, you will end up getting $1000 in face value when the bond matures, on top of whatever interest you get paid with your coupon rate.

Contrary to popular wisdom, you do not have to sell a stock when it skyrockets. Again, stocks are instruments that are meant to be held for five years minimum. So if it shoots up within six months, you should not feel any pressure to sell. If you think it is a good opportunity and you can put the excess money you make on selling the stock into another investment, then sell. If not, then hold it.

But When Do I Buy?

Quite honestly, you need to buy when you are able to lose whatever it is you invest. Like we have said before, and will say again, you need to understand that investing is like gambling. There is no guarantee that you will see your initial investment or any profits. So the first clue that you should buy stocks and bonds is when you are in a position to not miss the money that you are investing.

But you should also buy stocks when the market is either in a slump or when you feel like the stocks and the market is undervaluing bonds and stocks that you are trying to acquire. This will help you realize not only your initial investment but also profits in the long term. And that's what investing is all about – the long term.

Another indication of when to buy into an investment is when you see that the rate of return is particularly high. This will help you realize profits over the long term because it will pay out greater dividends compared to investments that have lower interest rates.

At the end of the day, you are going to have to use your intuition, your research, and advice from the experts to determine when to buy into a particular investment. But whatever you do, remember, don't follow the herd! Collectively, people usually act with poor judgment. So trust your gut and make the investments that you know will work for you and your goals.

In our next chapter, we will introduce you to the language of investing and hopefully make you feel a little more familiar with the terms that are commonly used by experts.

If you're enjoying this book please leave a review on Amazon, we love to hear feedback from readers!

Chapter 5: The Language of Investing

In this chapter, we are going to help break down the language barrier that exists between experienced investors and beginners. We promise it's not difficult. We are going to put everything in layman's terms with some examples so that you can see how things work in the real world. You will see that the investment world is really not so scary and complicated after all.

The Importance of a Good Mix of Assets

Your asset mix in your portfolio is going to help you manage your risk and also help maximize your return. An asset mix is the different kinds of assets in a portfolio that can be reduced to stocks, bonds, cash, and real estate.

Your mix will depend on what you can afford and how much risk you want in your portfolio. The more cash and bonds you have, the less risk you will have. The more stocks and real estate that you have in your portfolio, the more risk you will have. Contrary to popular belief, while real estate is a great investment, it is risky. If 2008 taught us anything, it is that real estate investing can turn ugly really quickly.

You or your broker will be able to create a good asset mix for you that will get you the kinds of returns that you desire.

Annual Yearly Percentage

This is your annual rate of return on your assets. This rate of return takes into account compound interest, which is the friend of investors everywhere. The reason this particular measurement of interest is useful is because whereas simple rates of return just tell you how much you get on your principal, the APY takes into account compound interest. This is a useful measure to compare different portfolios and investment tools.

A competitive rate will be one that, taking into account similar asset allocations and actual amount investment, will deliver more at the end of a fixed period of time. Here, you will need to do your homework and try to see that if everything else is held similar, you will get a higher rate of return for Fund X versus Fund Y.

Compensating for Your Risk-Level

You are going to want to be able to compensate for your level of risk. If you are the kind of person who feels like playing it fast and loose with your investments, then you are going to want to go a little heavier on the stocks and real estate portions of your funds. These types of investments will give you the highest rate of return for your investment while also exposing you to the greatest amount of risk.

But if you are a more conservative investor, you will want to invest more in bonds and then have more of your portfolio in cash. You will not earn as much in terms of rate of return, but you will have a more guaranteed rate of return and will have a lowered exposure to risk over the years.

Of course, if you are someone who is in between, then you will need to find a mix of conservative and risky. This is where it would be handy to go ahead and hire a broker. They will be able to give you the expert advice you need to make the right decisions for your future.

In our next chapter, we talk about people who did make those right decisions and reaped the rewards for years.

Chapter 6: Starting from Scratch: Warren Buffett Did It, So Can You!

In this chapter we are going to talk about the different investors from around the world who started with next to nothing and ended up making it big. You will probably recognize a few of the names on this list. The most important thing to remember about each of these people is that their success did not happen overnight: they put in the work and their hard work paid off in millions of dollars.

Warren Buffett

Warren Buffett of Berkshire Hathaway is probably the most famous investor in the world. He has give the populace investing advice for years and is also famously frugal. It might not surprise you that he had simple beginnings.

He was born at the very beginning of the Great Depression, to a mother who was a housewife and a father who was a stockbroker. Not rich by any means, Warren learned from an early age how to turn a profit. He used to buy six packs of soda from the grocery store and then sell them on the street corner for a profit. He would start lemonade stands and pocket all the money he ended up making. He wasn't a very fun kid, since when everyone else was having a good time playing hide and seek he was off trying to make money, but he was such a good saver that he was able to buy his first three shares of stock at the tender age of eleven.

That was his first foray into investing. By the time he was old enough to go to college, he had saved up $5,000 from a newspaper route. He didn't really want to go to college, but his parents urged him to go and eventually he did graduate from college. Funnily enough, after he graduated, he tried to go to graduate school at Harvard – and was rejected.

Undeterred, he went on to found the Buffettt Partnership and eventually took over Berkshire Hathaway. Nowadays, he is worth around $84 billion dollars. All of this happened because he decided at a young age to save what he had and invest it wisely. Of course, it does help that he can do crazy kinds of math in his head, but that being said, we can all learn a lot from Warren Buffettt:

- Save most of what you make.
- Invest those savings.
- Invest wisely – do not sell hastily!
- Never give up, even in the face of incredible odds.

Chris Gardner

Christ Gardner was made famous when Will Smith portrayed him in "The Pursuit of Happyness." Chris Gardner was a man (is a man) who had an entrepreneurial spirit from the start. Trying to sell medical equipment to doctors, he soon realized that he was fighting a losing battle. (It was essentially the 1980s version of a multi-level-marketing scam.) Then his partner left him and he very quickly found himself a single parent, without a job, and homeless. He needed to figure out what to do and fast.

There was no way that he and his son could continue to spend nights in homeless shelters and subway restrooms. So he applied and landed a Wall Street internship. I don't think I have to tell you that this, like other internships, was unpaid. But there would be a huge payoff for him if he just invested himself in the process. So taking side jobs along the way to keep himself and his son fed and clothed, he made his way up through the internship and landed a job as an investor with a major Wall Street firm.

He learned the value of risk and reward. He took a huge risk by taking an unpaid internship at literally the worst possible time in his life. But it paid off in literal millions. He now has several published books and has spent many years on Wall Street as a successful investor. His individual strategies don't really matter – what matters from his story is that we learn that sometimes the biggest risks can really end up paying off the most.

Some key takeaways from Chris Gardner:
- Take a chance on that unpaid internship.
- Have a goal and give it everything you've got.
- The biggest risks will yield the biggest rewards.
- Remember that investing is always a game of strategy.

Ken Langone

Now, you may think you don't know who Ken Langone is, but if you've ever walked into a Home Depot, you have him to thank.

He is the son of Italian immigrants, who actually dug ditches before going to college. While in college, he studied economics before joining the Army. After he got out of the army, he joined Wall Street and ended up putting his economics degree to good use. He took Electronic Data Systems public in 1968 and launched his career as one of the most successful investors of all time.

He ended up then making a small investment in Home Depot – we can clearly see how that investment turned out. He is also famous for his frugality. He doesn't go to Starbucks, he will call the cable company and argue over his bill – he won't even buy himself a bagel most days. He enjoys things like the theater and going out to dinner, but he takes joy in saving his money.

I think that, ultimately, is what we can take away from Ken's story. One, you need to understand that when you make an initial investment, it may be years before you see the payoff. I am sure that in 1978, when he made that initial investment in Home Depot, he had no idea that it would turn out this well. But he stuck with it and is now a multi-billionaire. Also, save, save, save. It is a lot of fun to get those dividend checks in the mail, but resist the urge to spend them! Save it and reinvest it. Remember, don't touch that money!

Key takeaways from Ken Langone:
- You are never too rich to argue with the cable company about your bill.
- Remember that Starbucks is not actually life – it's just coffee.
- Be patient – good things come to those who wait.
- Do not rob yourself by taking money out of your investments before they pay off!

Oprah Winfrey

If you are alive and well in 2018 and you do not know who Oprah Winfrey is, it might be time to crawl out from under your rock. I won't take you through a detailed biography of Ms. Winfrey, but I will tell you this: she was told at 23 that she would never make it in the media. She is now a multi-billionaire with an extremely successful media enterprise that will likely outlive all of us.

She learned that she had a gift and that it was up to her to never give up on it. She also knew that the investment she was making in herself was going to take years before she would see a payoff. She made the decision at 23 to keep trying and she didn't see the benefits of that risk until many years down the line. She never spent her money unwisely. (I mean, I'm sure she regretted some of her outfits, but I don't think those really count as unwise investments- more like poor choices in stylists.)

Some key takeaways from Oprah Winfrey's story:

- When people tell you that you can't do something, all they are really trying to do is make themselves feel better about not taking any chances in their life.

- Again, be patient! I'm sure at 23, she had no idea that would turn out to be a multi-billionaire.

- Invest in yourself first, always.

Andrew Carnegie

Our last billionaire is the famous Andrew Carnegie. Carnegie was an immigrant who came to the United States with nothing in his pockets in 1848. Carnegie built his fortune after spending years toiling away on the lower end of the totem pole. He ended up becoming a steel baron who built the American railway system as we know it. He was one of the richest Americans of his time and is constantly used as an example of the American industrial spirit – if he can forge himself into a billionaire from nothing, so can you. He not only was an industrialist, but he was an investor, too. He learned from a young age that if you invest your money wisely and hold onto those investments, it will pay off in the long run.

He had a rather famous philosophy on life that I think is worth sharing with you new investors. He was convinced that one should spend the first 33% of your life learning. Learn as much as you can in that time period, whether it be through school, working, or however else you can pack in the knowledge. The next third of your life should be spent chasing that paper. Make money, as much money as you possibly can during that time period. The last third, then, should be spent in the pursuit of philanthropy. Basically, do some good with all that money you made. He was a man who was convinced that wealth was supposed to be used to benefit all, not just one.

Some key takeaways from Andrew Carnegie:

- Learn everything you can while you have the ability.

- Make as much money as humanly possible.

- Do good with that money.

- Invest your money wisely.

- Hold on to those investments.

In the next chapter, we are going to discuss who you can trust when it comes to your hard-earned money.

Chapter 7: Who to Trust

Perhaps one of the most overlooked things to consider when people begin investing is thinking about who they should trust with their money. Obviously, we are assuming that you can trust yourself, but it is the rest of the world that we need to think about.

When you are thinking about choosing an investor, make sure you do your research. And we aren't just talking about a simple Google search, either. You really need to put in some effort at tracking these people down. Are they registered on FINRA's website? Do they have any complaints against them? Do they have any either open or closed legal matters that were pursued against them because of their actions? Do they have good testimonials on their website?

These are just a few of the questions that you need to consider when choosing a broker or an online trading platform. Remember the old adage: if it's too good to be true, it probably is.

Online Investors: The Wild West or Too Highly Regulated?

Here's the thing: with online investors, you really are at the mercy of whatever online disclosures you sign. It's kind of like those iTunes disclosures, right? You could be signing away your soul for all you know.

In reality, of course, you're not really signing away your soul. The key here is that when you use an online trading platform, you are the one in control. You don't have a broker that you are paying to make all of your buy, sell, and hold decisions. That is all on you. Obviously, there are going to be risks and rewards with that particular model. The risk is that you don't know what you are doing and you end up making terrible decisions. Those terrible decisions lead you to lose your money, your house, your wife...you get the picture.

But the reward is that you're not paying brokerage fees to a guy who gets paid to basically plug a bunch of numbers into a computer and do what it says. Because if you are not a high net worth investor, that's exactly what you're getting. See, because fees have so drastically decreased, brokers need to make money somehow, right? So they are going to go after the big fish. That's why you don't typically see commercials for Merrill Lynch on the Home Shopping Network. Those aren't exactly *their kind of people*, if you catch my drift.

Plus, along with big trading firms like that comes a literal ton of red tape. If you want a trade executed quickly, good luck. You first need to call your broker, who needs to fill out a form, who then needs to bring that form to management, who then needs to analyze the trade, then sign the form, make the appropriate copies, file those copies, then return the form and tell the broker that they can make the trade. It's absolutely insane sometimes. The reason for these regulations is definitely sound, as we will cover a little later in this chapter, but you really do face a whole lot of bureaucracy when you choose to go to a big firm like that.

If you want specialized attention, then you are going to have to be worth that attention. And in most brokers' minds, this means that you are going to need to be worth at least a quarter of a million dollars. I don't know about you, but when I first started out, I was not worth that much money. God bless my parents, but even they aren't worth that much money and they have been in the job market for decades longer than myself.

So you're going to need to weigh these options carefully. If you are not the kind of person who is already worth a ton of money, then you really might want to consider trying an online trading platform like E*Trade. You can lower your costs per trade and not pay a guy to input all your trades for you when you can simply do it yourself.

The Laws Governing The Broker

The Securities and Exchange Commission, or the SEC, as it is more commonly known, is the governing body that watches over stockbrokers and their ilk. It has long been understood that this is an industry that thrives on deregulation and wants to have as much room to move as possible. And that is completely understandable – after all, I just railed against the bureaucracy you face when you choose to put your money with a big firm. If they want to really be able to serve their clients quickly, then they need as little red tape as possible.

But what about serving their clients well? See, for a long time, brokers were able to charge absolutely enormous fees on investment accounts and these fees were dependent on the type of investments that the brokers chose. For example, if Stock A only paid a few dollars in fees for a broker versus Stock B, which would produce hundreds of dollars worth of fees, the broker would pick Stock B, regardless of the consequences for the client.

This is obviously irresponsible and unethical behavior. Especially when it's concerning someone's retirement. Someone trusts this person with their livelihood, something that they have spent their entire lives working on earning. It is also money that they are depending on to get them through their retirement comfortably. It is a hard blow when that person who was trusted with such a sacred responsibility acts on selfish impulse.

So the SEC imposed a new rule. If a broker was to be handling a retirement account (which is about 90% of the accounts that they handle) then they were to become fiduciaries.

Fiduciaries are charged with a legal obligation to always do what is in the best interest of the client. This means that if Stock A is the better choice but will result in less fees for the broker, the broker must choose Stock A because that is what is in the client's best interest. So many of the big brokerage firms fought back against this rule because they didn't want any more red tape, but people were tired to being taken advantage of. And so the law passed.

Now, if you charge a broker with the responsibility of helping you secure their retirement, you can rest assured that they absolutely must act in your best interests or face very serious consequences – from heavy fines to even imprisonment.

Now, for an example of a life-cycle of an investment:

Let's quickly walk through a sample investment so that you can get a feel of what it's like in the real world. Let's say that you have $1000 that you have saved up and you finally want to jump in on this investment game. First, good for you! Excellent choice.

With that $1000, you should seriously consider looking into a mutual fund. This will get you the most bang for your buck and will allow you to shift your investment allocations as your needs change and you get closer to retirement. Let's say that you pick Vanguard. Again, excellent decision, as it has one of the best rates of return on the market today.

Decide on your asset mix – I would go with a 40% stock and 60% bond and other securities to keep things on the safer side. If you are younger, though, say in your mid-to-late twenties, maybe take a riskier approach. You have a long road ahead of you in the investment world, so you have the time (literally) to ride out the storms.

Now, just wait and adjust as you wait. Say that the economy takes a bit of a dive. Evaluate, see where you can hold, what you should dump, and what you should buy. Buying during an economic slump can be a good idea because stock prices are going to be lower than they would be normally. When the market picks up again, reevaluate. See what you can sell for a profit and then reinvest those profits to shift your risk allocation to your needs at the time.

And just keep waiting. After about ten years or so, you will need to do a serious reallocation and perhaps think about just getting out of that fund entirely and putting the money that you have made into an annuity or other kind of investment. Because here's the thing: when you are younger, you have more time to recover from a disastrous market cycle. You need to be more aggressive the younger you are – this will require you to steel yourself a bit, because like we have discussed before, investing is not for the faint of heart. You will need to realize that there are times when investing that you are just going to have to white-knuckle your way through.

But as you get older, you need a portfolio that has less risk. Retirement is not the time to bet the whole pot on a crazy business venture or on a bond that has a terrible credit rating. Readjust as you age and as you get more stock-market savvy. This will pay off for you in the long run. Also, make sure that you are consistently adding and reinvesting your dividends into your mutual fund. This will help you take advantage of that compound interest. Compound interest is the best friend you will ever have, outside of your dog.

The Dangers of Being a Lemming

Sure, lemmings are kinda cute. They are like fuzzy little arctic meerkats. But they are also really, really, really dumb. They tend to just follow whatever the lemming in front of them is doing. This is great if there is a lemming conga line, but really bad if the lemming in front of you decides to jump off a cliff.

So what the heck does this have to do with you? A lot, actually. One of the biggest mistakes new investors (or any kind of investor, really) can make is deciding to just follow the herd and adjust your portfolio to whatever is in fashion at the time. That is a really good way to lose a lot of money and waste your time constantly adjusting your portfolio. Don't worry about what the crowd is doing —you know what your goals are; just keep those in mind and do your own thing. Warren Buffettt didn't get rich by playing hopscotch like all the other kids. Take a leaf from his book.

Chapter 8: How to Win at the Stock Market Game

Here is where we get to talk about some of the fun stuff: how to make it really big by playing the stock market. Keep in mind that again, any time you invest, you are taking a risk. Also, we do not know your financial situation or risk tolerance – if you have any questions or feel like you need to talk it through, find an advisor near you and see what they have to say.

Winning: Not Just for Charlie Sheen

What are some overarching strategies that you, the new investor, can use when it comes to making it big on the stock market? Here are just a few insights:

1. Diversify: this is a big one. We have all heard the story about not all of your eggs in one basket. Well, this is true for investments as well. You don't want to have a portfolio that is all stocks, or all bonds, or all cash. Or even all ETFs, (exchange traded funds) as handy as they are. If you put all of your investments in one basket and that basket springs a leak, you are straight out of luck. If you diversify your portfolio, you are automatically reducing your risk.

   a. As we have discussed above, reducing your risk is going to help you as you get closer to retirement, but you don't need to be quite as concerned about it when you first start out.

2. Balance, rebalance, and rebalance again: If you want to be successful in investing, you are going to need to brush up on your math skills. No, you aren't going to need to become a rocket scientist overnight, but you are going to need to embrace the mathematical side of investing. This means you will need to examine the risks of your stocks, measure them against the money that you are willing to lose, and then figure out if it's worth it. There is quite a bit more math that is involved, if we are being honest, but for now, as a beginner, just understand that you are going to need to invest more than just your money

when you start investing – you are going to need to invest your time.

3. Work with either a broker or an online trading program that allows you to have more than one set of eyes on your investments: after all, you are just one person. And unless you are a day trader who spends literally 100% of their time while the markets are open watching and waiting and trading, you are going to need to be doing other things with your time. Set up your dashboard on your online accounts to send you notifications when stocks that you had your eye on become available, or when certain bonds are being sold at a discount. If you automate as much of the process as you can, then you will be able to be that much more successful.

4. Speaking of day trading: it's another way you can win at the stock market. The reason it's called day trading is because every trade that you make will be completed within that time frame. Usually reserved for professionals, this particular strategy is now more beginner-friendly because of services like AmeriTrade and E*Trade.

5. Position trading: remember how we talked about stock market investing being a long-term kind of a thing? Well, this reinforces that idea. When you are position trading, you are buying and holding different types of securities. This is a little bit more of an advanced strategy, though, because when you are position trading, you are trying to read how the market is going to react in the future. You will need formulas and charts and different kinds of markers to determine how you will invest now so that it can pay off in the future. It's complicated, but definitely worth the effort. If you want more information on how to do this and who to talk to, head on over to Investopedia. They can hook you up with detailed strategies and direct you to some excellent brokers who can lead you in the right direction.

6. Swing trading: no, this isn't nearly as much fun as it sounds. It involves quite a bit of math because you need to act quickly to buy and sell during a very short period of time. When there is volatility in the market because either an upswing or downturn has begun or ended, you have an opportunity to make some money. You will need to develop some algorithms to figure out when to buy and sell. Again, this is a more advanced investment strategy for folks who have been around the investment block, but it's something worth discussing with your broker.

7. Scalping: okay, so this probably sounds like the worst strategy ever, right? Well, again, this is a time-is-of-the-essence kind of strategy. You are essentially trying to take advantage of a gap in between the ask and sell price. This again, is a more advanced strategy, but something worth looking into as you get more familiar with the stock market.

Value Investing

I think we have probably talked enough about the advanced strategies for now, so we will move on to the kind of investment strategies that you can bring with you the first time you set up a trade. The first type of investing we would like to talk about is value investing. Value investing is incredibly simple and just requires some time, patience, and of course, some capital.

Value investing is the same principle you use when you go to the store and see that your favorite wine is on sale. You know that this bottle of wine is normally priced at $50, but for today only, you can get it for $35! You, the savvy shopper that you are, knows that you are getting a great deal – you are paying only $35 for a bottle of wine that is easily worth $50 on any other day of the week. So you pounce and you buy up several bottles.

The next day, you walk into the same store (because of course you forgot something, like 99% of people who go to the grocery store) and you see people happily buying up bottles of that $50 wine at full price. You smile to yourself, knowing that you got a great deal. That, in a nutshell, is value investing. But I am sure that you are going to want a few more specifics, so here you go – the principles of value investing:

1. You understand that companies, like wine, have a basic value. You know that when you are buying wine, it has an inherent value. Well, so do companies. If you understand that well, you can snap up stock when the market isn't valuing that stock as it should and get it at a massive discount. Then, when the market gets its act together and properly values the company at what it's worth, you can sell your stock and make a large profit. Sounds pretty great, right?

2. Always have a cushion. No, this isn't a tip for how to keep yourself comfy during your day-trading hours. You need to make sure that when you are valuing these stocks, you have enough money in play that if you are wrong and mistakenly value the stock at higher than what it should be, you won't lose your shirt. It seems obvious, but you would be surprised how many people walk a razor thin line between winning it big and losing everything they have. The point of this book is not to teach you how to be a reckless investor, but how to be a winning investor. Winning investors understand that they can make mistakes and insure against those mistakes by making sure they have a cash cushion at the ready. Be like a winner: keep a cushion.

3. You understand that sometimes the market is wrong about a stock. You know that the Dow and the Standard and Poor 500 indexes are not always right about a stock. If you know, deep down, and hopefully based on some solid numbers, that a particular stock is undervalued by the market at this point in time, then you should act on that instinct and buy it at what you perceive to be a discount. That is the only way you can then reap the reward when the market corrects itself and then values the stock at its proper price.

4. Don't be a lemming! We have talked about this before. Successful value investors understand that more often than

not, the herd, or the crowd, is wrong. Just like your mother said, if your friends were jumping off of a bridge, would you join them? I don't think so. Just remember that the herd isn't always right. Follow your instincts, follow your plan, and do what is best for you and you only.

Growth Investing

This is a fairly intuitive style of investing, though it is slightly riskier than value investing. Growth investing focuses on stocks or companies who they believe are going to outpace the market in terms of growth. Basically, these kinds of investors think that they have the ticket to the top and bet it all on companies that they think are going to experience massive growth. The problem here is that no one has a crystal ball. So if you turn out to be wrong, you have the potential to ruin your finances and leave yourself with those tumbleweeds we talked about earlier, rolling through your bank account. But if you find a smaller company that you feel is destined for big things or you find a new market that nobody has invested in yet, then maybe you have a chance at making it big.

Take a look at works by Peter Lynch and Thomas Rowe Price, Jr., if you want to take a deeper insight into how this kind of investing works. Both of them are notable names in the investing world and have specifically worked on this kind of investing.

Of course, this is the type of investing that it would be useful to bring up with a real live broker. If you have reached this kind of investment model and are ready to start taking bigger risks and investing bigger sums of money, it would be worthwhile to go to a big trading house and see if you can get a broker. You'd also be surprised at the amount of financial planners that exist right in your hometown. A simple Google search will often yield a plethora of financial planners who are excited to help you build your future. Obviously, again, you will need to do your research here. See if they are registered with FINRA, if there are any complaints against them – see what their customers have to say. If they don't have any testimonials on their website and their registration on FINRA is littered with complaints, you are probably going to want to stay far away from that planner. But you can find a good one and I encourage you to do so once you have reached this level of investing.

Income Investing

So, this is a great type of investment for people who want to keep a steady stream of income into their bank account while still having money invested. Typically, for this type of investment, you are going to want to pick bonds that generate steady returns and have good credit ratings. But there are also stocks out there that will pay you regular dividends as well.

This type of investing is good for people who can't tie up a whole bunch of money in illiquid investments because they have other things going on like car payments, a mortgage, and kids. It will help avoid messy situations where you need cash and can't sell your stocks quickly enough in an emergency situation.

Just remember that companies are not required to pay out dividends regularly. You are going to want to do your homework on this and see what companies out there make enough of a profit to actually pay dividends and which ones do so on a regular basis. While this type of investing is not going to jet set you into millionaire status overnight, it is a nice way of supplementing your current income so that maybe you can go on vacation or cover that car repair without having to go into debt.

So what are some good income investments for you? Well, that's why you bought this book! So take a look below for some income investment strategies that will help you out:

First, take a look at money market funds. These are funds that are extremely safe – you won't have to worry too much about losing your initial investment. These funds pay out nice dividends, but will not make you rich, by any stretch of the imagination. This should not be your only source of income. What you should do with these returns is reinvest them either in that same fund or elsewhere in your total investment portfolio.

CDs, or certificates of deposit, are another great way to produce income for yourself without much, if any, risk. The idea here is that you deposit a certain amount of money into a certificate of deposit and then you wait for it to grow and grow before you cash it out. Certificates of deposits are not meant to be super long term investments, but what they do not offer in longevity, they do offer in great interest rates and no risk. See, each deposit you make into a certificate of deposit is protected by the FDIC and you are protected up to $250,000 in aggregate.

Let's walk through a certificate of deposit so you can see how it works. Most banks require a $5,000 deposit to open up one of these accounts. Say it offers you a six percent interest rate that compounds quarterly. And if you're smart, which we know you are because you're reading this book, you will make consistent investments every month. But even if you don't, if you just leave that five thousand dollars in that account for five years, you will have $6,734 ready for you when you cash out. Now that's pretty amazing. And it's a strong argument for opening up one of these accounts and putting your money in one.

Bonds are another great way to get some income from your investments. As a refresher, these are little bits of debt that you have bought from either a company or Uncle Sam. You are going to get paid when the bond matures and as the coupon rate indicates – this is your interest rate, remember? So if your coupon rate is 5%, you will get paid five percent either each year you hold the bond or however often that coupon percentage is paid out.

Mutual funds that are made of bonds and exchange traded funds (ETFs): these kinds of portfolios will give you much more income than just holding several individual bonds. This type of portfolio will help you diversify across many different markets while increasing the number of payouts you receive.

This means that each of you owns a different percentage of the mutual fund and will receive your payments accordingly. So someone who has put five thousand dollars into the fund will of course receive greater dividends than someone who has invested one thousand. But you will all be invested in the same stocks and bonds, just in different amounts. So how do you earn money? Well, same as you would on a regular investment. You will earn dividends on your stocks and if you sell a security that has gone up in price, then you will earn a profit. And finally, let's say that those same securities increase in price but you don't sell the individual securities. You can just sell off portions of your mutual fund. You can then reap the profits from that.

The top three mutual funds for your retirement are Vanguard Institutional Index I, American Funds Euro Pacific Growth F1, and Fidelity Freedom 2030. Vanguard, over a ten-year period, will earn you

7.5%. Over that same time period, American Funds will earn you 3.0% and Fidelity will earn you 4.4%. These are all incredibly competitive rates of return and are worth examining further.

Finally, you can look into closed-end funds. A closed-end fund is similar to a mutual fund, except that it is for one specific company that is looking to raise money through an initial public offering, or an IPO. These are attractive to new investors because sometimes you can get in on the ground floor of the next Google or Facebook. That would probably be the ultimate income investment, right? But there is no guarantee in this or any kind of investment. And while I am sure that you are very tired of hearing me tell you to do research, it really is an important part of being a savvy investor. Sign up for newsletters, read the Skimm, take a look around the dusty corners of the internet – the more knowledge you have about what is happening in the stock market, the better chance you have of making a killing.

Passive Investing

Who doesn't like to just have money appear in their bank account? I know I love it when that happens. Basically, you are not spending all your time buying and selling when you are on this strategy, you are going to make sure that your returns are maximized by reducing the costs that are associated with constant buying and selling. This is the slow and steady approach to investing.

The whole idea here is that if you are patient and willing to ride through the storms, over time you will see positive growth in your portfolio. Ideally, you will have a well-diversified portfolio that does well with market risk and the odd downturn here and there. You are not trying to outpace the market or day trade your way to wealth with passive investing. You are literally just setting it and forgetting it.

While we are on the subject of passive investing, let's talk a little bit about passive income. It's basically the same thing, right? Well, sort of. Passive income is where you do something like install a plugin on your blog or set up an affiliate link on your website that earns you money whenever someone clicks that link. Honestly, these are some of the easiest ways to earn money with as little effort as possible. You can also do things like take online surveys, sign up for a service like Acorns, which rounds up your online purchases and deposits the change into an account, or even just give yourself a dollar every time you pass Starbucks and don't buy a cup of coffee. These are all ways to help build up a little bit of wealth that you can then invest and make work for you.

Because that's really the point, isn't it? You want to make your money work for you. After all, you spend over one third of your life at work, trying to make money. It only makes sense that you would then demand that your money work for you. This is why passive investing makes so much sense for beginners. Instead of running around like a chicken with your head cut off, trying to find investments that are going to earn you money if you buy and then sell and then reinvest, or trying to figure out if the new company you invested all your savings into is going to go public *any minute now*, you can just set up a steady stream of investments that will pay you handsome dividends without you having to lift a finger. It will help you get used to investing and get you some valuable experience so that later, you can take more control of your investments.

To that end, I am going to give you four great examples of passive investments that can really give you the bang for your buck that you deserve.

First, real estate! No, I'm not saying that you're going to become the next Donald Trump. Even if you wanted to, which is totally up to you, it's not really guaranteed that this type of passive investment will catapult you into billionaire status. However, it is one of the easiest ways to continually reap rewards without putting in too much effort. Basically, you buy a piece of real estate – a duplex, a home, maybe even an apartment complex. And you rent it out. Simple as that. Obviously you will need to take care of things for the tenants, or have a management company handle that for you, but this is definitely one kind of investment where you can buy it and then forget about it.

You can also invest in real estate even if you can't afford an actual brick and mortar residence. In this increasing digital age, you are now able to invest in real estate digitally. What do I mean by that? Think of it like investing in a mutual fund, but just one that is focused on real estate. These are called real estate investment trusts, or, REITs. You just invest in the fund and you don't have to worry about someone's clogged toilet or if a roof has a leak. You just enjoy those dividends.

Crowdfunding for real estate is also a very real thing nowadays. Through websites like Ground Floor, you can get in at literally the very beginning of a real estate project and reap the rewards. It works like any other crowd funding website where you put up whatever money you can, and that is your share of the project. Then you get dividends based on how much money you invested. The crowd funding real estate market is interesting because you are not putting money into a fund, per se, but are actually funding the loan that allows people to buy a house. When these people get a mortgage, it is thanks to your contribution. So see, you can do a good thing for someone (i.e., helping them buy a house) and do something good for yourself – pay yourself some cash money!

Second, you can look into peer-to-peer lending. This is ideal for initial investors who are trying to up their capital while also earn some money. It is a similar idea to the real estate crowd funding – you put up some money on a loan and then get paid depending on your investment. Obviously, too, if you give money to someone who is a bigger credit risk, you are going to get a bigger return interest-wise. So take a chance, loan somebody a few bucks, and then earn some money yourself. It could turn out well.

Next, dividend stocks! As the name suggests, these are stocks that pay regular dividends. As we have mentioned before, not all companies do this! You are going to want to research and see what companies are most noted for paying out dividends regularly. Johnson and Johnson is a particularly well-known company that does pay out dividends to its investors on a fairly regular basis. But you are going to have to put in some time and research the companies that you can count on for your passive income. Passive income isn't just literally waiting for the money to fall into your lap – you do need to put in a little work on the front end of things.

Also, take a chance on index funds. As we have mentioned before, these are mutual funds whose performance is tied to a particular market, like the Dow or the Standard and Poor 500. The better that those indexes do, the better your returns will be. You just have to set up a well-diversified portfolio and let things lie.

Take a look at high yield savings accounts. So, your bank is likely going to be able to offer you some sort of low-interest account, but it's really going to not give you a whole lot of extra money in the long run. You're going to take a look at these high yield savings accounts that exist. They really are an easy way to not only save money consistently, but also a way to make sure that your money is working for you in a zero-risk environment.

One of the best high yield savings accounts out there can be found with Synchrony Bank. (Remember that movie, Thor: Ragnarok? They were actually featured on a cab in the background. Not really investment related and certainly not the main reason why you should invest your money with them, but it is a cool little factoid. Anyway, back to high yield savings accounts.) Synchrony offers you a 1.90% APY, which blows most bank savings account interest rates out of the water.

Other high yield savings accounts include Discover, CIT Bank, Barclay's, American Express, and Marcus, by Goldman Sachs. Each of them offers 1.90% as well, but each one will have different requirements regarding an initial deposit and a minimum balance. The nice thing about Synchrony is that you can set up your online transfers on a specific date to go forward on a rolling basis and can adjust the amount you are saving with just a click of a button. It's pretty awesome. So take a chance and look into a high yield savings account. You can save money and "invest" at the same time without worrying that you are going to lose your initial investment – remember, deposits in banks are FDIC insured up to $250,000.

Robo advisors are another way for you to invest in a more passive way. This is an amazing option for people who do not have the time to go and talk to a broker or go and sit in front of their computer for ten hours a day and learn how to be a day trader. So, robo advisors are little bots on the internet that will take your money (at a pre-set time and amount) and invest it for you. What's cool about this option is that your time up-front is basically about ten minutes. You tell the little robots a little bit about yourself, you fork over some cash, and they then go and invest your money for you.

Obviously, there are layers of code and other technical things that are going on here, but this is such a great opportunity for first-time investors to get their feet wet and also make sure that you are not paying more than is absolutely necessary in fees. Remember, we don't like fees. They take away our hard-earned money. Money that could be earning you more money while you sleep. We don't like fees.

If you want to check out robo advisors, head on over to Betterment. Those folks will be able to set you up quickly and get you ready to invest. Across the industry, they charge the lowest fees for this kind of service. So you will get expert advice on investments at a literal fraction of the cost.

Another opportunity for passive investing that we would like to discuss before we move on is the idea of investing in a small business. Apple was started in a garage. Lyft was started because a guy thought that he could offer a better service than cabs and just use his own car. Those companies are now worth billions. The people who were able to get in on the ground floor reaped their investment many times over. I'm not saying that every small business has the potential to be the next Google, Apple, or Lyft, but you never know.

Just remember that you will not see the benefits of your investment right away. It may take many years before you are able to see a return on your investment. This is because in order for you to receive any sort of repayment, the company that you invested in will either need to sell through an initial public offering (IPO) or be bought by another, bigger company. But it can happen! Just do your homework, lead with your gut, and watch that money tree grow.

At the end of the day, this is about making sure that you have money coming into your bank account that you can save and reinvest. It is about putting in minimal effort and ensuring maximum return. Who doesn't like that?

Chapter 9: Advanced Strategies and Success Stories

All right, so now it's time for the fun stuff. In this chapter, we are going to talk about some of the more advanced strategies that the pros use to make them some serious change on the stock market. Remember, though, that these strategies are for people who have been doing this for a while. We do not recommend trying to figure out how to short sell stock on your very first investment foray. But take a look at what we've got going on here and keep it in mind for down the road.

In this chapter we are going to discuss short-selling, buying on the margin, day-trading (sound familiar?) and portfolio management. We are also going to give you some success stories of the people who have used some of these strategies to make it big on Wall Street. So, here we go!

Short-selling

This is probably the sexiest topic in the stock-market world. Everyone and their mother wants to talk about shorting a stock. This is because if you do it right and you do it ethically, you could potentially earn billions of dollars. Yes, I said billions. Later on in this chapter we are going to talk about the guys who figured out how to short the housing market in 2008, when everything was crashing down around them, and walked away with billions of dollars. Of course, everyone else suffered, but we are trying to focus on the winners here.

Okay, so remember how we have been telling you that stocks are for long-term investing? Well, for this section, just try to forget that little tidbit. When you are trying to short-sell a stock, you are betting that the stock you're looking at is going to take a sharp decline in value. The best part about this is that you are betting on stock declining that *you don't actually own.*

But wait a minute – how can you make money on stock that's not your own? Great question! So, you do this by borrowing the stock from another investor, selling it at the current market price, and putting the sales proceeds into a margin account. Then, in the future, the person who is going to short the stock "covers" that shorted position in his margin account by buying the stock in the market and then repaying the person he borrowed the stock from in the first place. Sound confusing yet? Yeah, it's because it can be. Keep reading for a thorough example of what a short-selling transaction looks like:

You take a look at Company B. This Company looks a little bit like Tesla did before Elon Musk's famous 4/20 tweet that tanked their stock price: juicy, but with a hint of danger. You see that B's stock is currently selling for $100 per share. You decide that you want to short-sell this stock.

Your first order of business is to announce via your online trading platform that the stock you are buying is stock you are intending to short. For reasons that we will get into later, it is illegal to hide this fact from the market. So, you execute your buy and make sure that you have the legally required $25,000 in your margin account to cover whatever losses you may incur if you have made a mistake.

Let's say that you want to buy 10 shares. Your online broker will go and try to borrow those shares from other shareholders. Those shares are then deposited into your account. Now, the waiting game begins. You need to see if that stock does in fact decline in value and then immediately act when it does. So let's say that you wait a month and the stock declines to $75 per share. Buy and buy now! You buy back those ten shares at $75 per share, or $750. You repay the borrowers with that same stock that used to be worth $1000, and you net: $250. The equation is as follows ($100-$75) X 10. Pretty cool, right? Except for the fact that you needed to make sure you had the twenty five thousand dollars in your margin account. So you'd want to pick a stock that will net you a larger profit, but I think you get the idea.

Now remember, this strategy can also work against you. If you are wrong and the stock instead appreciates in value – you can be out thousands upon thousands of dollars. So make sure you are doing your homework before you try to short a stock. And because of the legal implications, I would very seriously recommend doing this type of transaction through a registered dealer who knows the laws and knows what they are doing to help prevent any sort of disaster.

Buying on the Margin

This is an extremely advanced strategy of investing. Basically, you are using credit to buy stocks. Sounds complicated? That is because it usually is. While it does allow you more freedom to buy stocks that you perhaps could not afford normally, it is a rather risky strategy.

So, let's say you want to buy Stock X, but you don't have the available cash to do so. If you have $20,000 in your margin account and you put up half of the purchase price of the stock, you have $40,000 that you can use to invest. So if you buy $10,000 worth of Stock X, you still have $30,000 that you can use to cover your trade without using your margin balance.

The problem with this is if you pick the wrong stock and it tanks then not only do you have to pay back what you borrowed, but you may have to dip into your margin account to cover the additional costs. Buying on the margin is extremely risky and really should only be done when you have either enough expertise and money to do it on your own or when you have taken the big leap and have hired a broker to do the sweating and the trading and the worrying for you.

Portfolio Management

Here's where you bring it all home. Portfolio management is about putting everything you have learned about stocks, bonds, and investments in general and making it work for you. Here are a few tips to guide you along the way:

1. Pay yourself first and pay yourself early. Make sure that when you receive your paycheck, you are setting aside money to invest. Make this the first thing you do every time you get a check – even if it's a check for your birthday. And start as soon as possible. If we learned anything from Warren Buffettt, it's that it is never too early to start paying ourselves.

2. Take risks in the beginning: remember, when you are younger, you have more time to recover from a disastrous day or two in the stock market. Take advantage of your youth and take a chance on some riskier ventures – remember that the biggest risks will have the biggest payoffs. As you get older, you can reallocate your risk and make things a little more conservative as you get older and get closer to retirement.

3. Diversify! As we have said before: this is a big one. We have all heard the story about not putting all of your eggs in one basket. Well, this is true for investments as well. You don't want to have a portfolio that is all stocks, or all bonds, or all cash. Or even all ETFs, (exchange traded funds) as handy as they are. If you put all of your investments in one basket and that basket springs a leak, you are straight out of luck. If you diversify your portfolio, you are automatically reducing your risk.

   a. As we have discussed above, reducing your risk is going to help you as you get closer to retirement, but you don't need to be quite as concerned about it when you first start out.

4. Asset allocation: Your asset mix in your portfolio is going to help you manage your risk and also help maximize your return. An asset mix is the different kinds of assets in a portfolio that can be reduced to stocks, bonds, cash, and real estate.

   a. Your mix will depend on what you can afford and how much risk you want in your portfolio. The more cash and bonds you have, the less risk you will have. The more stocks and real estate that you have in your portfolio, the more risk you will have. Contrary to popular belief, while real estate is a great investment, it is risky. If 2008 taught us anything, it is that real estate investing can turn ugly really quickly.
   b. You or your broker will be able to create a good asset mix for you that will get you the kinds of returns that you desire. Again, remember that your asset mix will change as you get older. When you are younger, you can take a little bit more risk in your portfolio. But as you get older, you will want to make sure that you are making asset allocations that are in line with the goal of having enough money in retirement. You don't want to take the risk of losing your hard-earned money when you are just about to retire.

5. Balance, rebalance, and rebalance again: If you want to be successful in investing, you are going to need to brush up on your

math skills. No, you aren't going to need to become a rocket scientist overnight, but you are going to need to embrace the mathematical side of investing. This means you will need to examine the risks of your stocks, measure them against the money that you are willing to lose, and then figure out if it's worth it. There is quite a bit more math that is involved, if we are being honest, but for now, as a beginner, just understand that you are going to need to invest more than just your money when you start investing – you are going to need to invest your time.

6. Consistency and taxes: make sure you are consistently paying yourself first. And consistently adding to your investments. Also, you are going to need to be mindful of the tax consequences of whatever income you earn from your investments. They are going to be subject to taxes, so it might be worth your time to consult with a tax expert when tax season comes around.

Success Stories

A little while ago we ran through some of the more famous investors in America, and we will include a refresher at the end of this chapter. But first, we would like to take this opportunity to discuss the success story of those guys who ended up figuring out how to short the housing market back in 2008. Remember those guys? Maybe not, because these guys managed to walk away from one of the biggest financial crises in history with their pockets full.

In 2008, the United States' housing market crashed. Hard. People defaulted on their mortgages left and right and the banks were hit hard when that happened. To give a little bit of context, it is important to remember that before the crash, mortgages and loans were being handed out like candy. People who were unable to afford groceries were being given the keys to mansions. To most people with common sense, it wasn't that big of a surprise when they were unable to keep up with their mortgage payments. But the big banks and lending companies didn't care.

See, they were taking these mortgages and using them as collateral for other investment securities around the world. So these giant trades were taking place with these shaky loans used as collateral. Thus, when the money stopped flowing into the mortgages because people just couldn't afford them, all of those securities suddenly collapsed. Imagine the mortgage like a big hot air balloon carrying a basket full of people over wine country. As long as that balloon stays full, everybody is safe and happy. But once that balloon goes flat, you're screwed. Well, that's exactly what happened with the housing market. People stopped blowing into the mortgage balloon and it dropped.

And it's not like nobody could see this coming. It doesn't take a genius to figure out that if someone can't afford their monthly groceries, they probably can't afford to be living in a Beverly Hills mansion. But yet, there they were, being given loans at crazy low interest rates. And so there were some people who were able to see ahead of the game and see that this was a literal disaster waiting to happen. Michael Burry, a hedge fund manager, saw it and prepared for years – he was able to short the housing market and walk away a billionaire. Mark Baum, another investment professional, saw it coming too and was able to invest with Michael Burry. He, too, walked away with billions. There are other players too, but those were the two biggest.

And both were ridiculed at first. Nobody believed that the 2008 crisis was going to happen – and yet it did and took years to recover. We still aren't back to 100% and experts are predicting another crash in the near future. So keep an eye out on things – like we said before, if something is too good to be true, it likely is. If you start seeing things like loans being given out as if they were on sale and people who have no business living in mansions all of a sudden living in mansions, maybe think about trying to short the market.

As always, remember that the investment market is a game. It's like playing blackjack – sometimes you win, sometimes you lose. It is not for the faint of heart or the weak of stomach. You need to be willing to lose whatever it is you invest, because the likelihood of you making it big is just as credible as the likelihood of you losing your investment. So what should you take away from these guys and their big win? Pay attention, hold on, and do not follow the herd! The herd mentality is what will end up costing you big bucks if you follow it. Remember, everybody told these guys that they were crazy – clients left them, their personal lives were a mess, and they were hemorrhaging money for a while. But it all paid off big. And it was mostly because they didn't listen to the herd, to the crowd, who told them that they were crazy. Stay true to your investment instincts and it can lead you far.

And since we promised, here is that refresher on other successful people who started at the bottom and made it big because they believed in themselves, invested wisely, and stayed the course, even during the hard times:

John Templeton

I am going to guess that you have never heard of this guy. Trust me, this will be a common theme as we explore some of the most successful American investors. These are guys who have made millions, sometimes billions, but who aren't on the front page of the newspaper. It seems like these guys value their privacy almost as much as they value their stock options. But let's begin.

John Templeton was born in 1912, and would go on to experience the Roaring Twenties and the Great Depression. Through it all, he managed to keep his head above water and ended up going to Yale University. He earned a degree there and eventually earned a law degree from Oxford, in England.

The reason we included him in this particular section of the book is because this is a man who weathered the storm of the greatest economic crisis this country has ever seen and ended up becoming one of the most successful investment fund managers in the world. He is the man who was the model of "buy low, sell high" and followed this strategy for almost his entire investment career. I guess if you were able to white-knuckle it through the Great Depression, waiting for your investments to pan out is probably a walk in the park.

Takeaways from John Templeton:

- Buy low, sell high (if it makes sense, of course).
- Hang on to your investments.
- Remember that investments are always a risk.

Philip Fisher

No, this is not the guy behind Fisher Price, but nice guess. Instead, Philip Fisher was a business-school dropout who became a millionaire on the back of his investment philosophy. Like Templeton, he began his career right at the tail end of the Roaring Twenties and just before the Great Depression. So not exactly a great time to be entering the stock market. But he did it anyway!

Fisher liked to invest in companies that focused on innovative research and technology. He was also famous for his tight-fisted approach to investing. I don't mean that he wasn't willing to let go of his money to invest it. What I mean by that is he bought one of his first stocks in 1955 and never sold it. How's that for commitment? And in case you were wondering, that stock was Motorola. He also followed the Templeton philosophy of buying low and selling high, when he did in fact sell.

He tended to pick his investments based on a personal fifteen-item checklist. Parts of that checklist included the characteristics of the company, but also included characteristics of the management. He believed that investing in a company required a multi-faceted approach to find out as much about the company as humanly possible before sinking money into it. It seems like common sense, but so many people invest blindly that it does bear repeating here.So remember those parts of this book where we kept harping on you to do your homework before you invest? Yeah, turns out we learned that from someone – and that someone was Philip Fisher.

Takeaways from Philip Fisher:

- Do your homework on the companies you are investing in!
- Hold on to your stocks – ride that rollercoaster.
- Develop your own investment checklist.

Benjamin Graham

Remember that famous guy we talked about before? Warren Buffettt? Yeah, Benjamin Graham was his mentor. According to Warren Buffettt, everything he learned about being a successful investor came from Graham. Buffettt has never faltered in his praise of Graham, and that alone could earn him a place on our list of success stories, even though his standalone accomplishments are many.

For example, he was a successful businessman before the Great Depression hit and he lost most of his money after that stock market crash. Yet he was able to take what he learned from that experience and turn it into cash. The first thing he did was write a best-selling book about the experience of risking his money in the stock market and then losing it all.

One of the more genius theories he had about investing was treating the stock market as if it were a sentient being. So, his theory was this: the stock market was like someone coming up to you and asking if you wanted to be his (or her!) business partner. You had the opportunity that day to do business with them or not. You didn't have to do anything at all. This is because the next day, that person will show up again. But this time, they may be in a different outfit and have a different business plan that will work out better for you. Just remember that – you have to treat the stock market like a person that you are going into business with.

Imagine all the searches you would run, the numbers you would crunch, the profiles you would stalk in order to find out as much as you could about that mysterious person who wants to do business with you. I mean, you don't know this person from Adam – what makes you think you can trust them with your money? Do they have a lot of debt? Do they have a history of leaving business partners high and dry? Or do they treat their partners will and pay them their fair share? Now treat the stock market like that person and you'll make some good choices. Because just like you wouldn't loan your money to a friend who you know is a flake, you wouldn't invest in a stock that you know won't pay off in the end.

Takeaways from Benjamin Graham:

- Take the stock market day by day.
- Do your research!
- Take failures and turn them into successes.

George Soros

If you watch the news at all, which you probably do, you will recognize this name. He is a rather famous investor who is very good at getting politicians very, very angry at him. But he has so much money, that I am fairly sure that whenever he gets demonized by a particular politician, he literally laughs on his way to the bank.

Fun fact about George Soros: he used the technique of short selling to effectively break the bank of England. He was the reason why the Queen suddenly had to pull out her Capital One Credit card to pay for her tea and scones. All kidding aside, he literally was able to short the British pound and caused a huge ruckus in the European financial markets. He ended up making over $1 billion in profit from that particular strategy. That's definitely "I'm laughing on the way to cash this check" money.

He was not always a billionaire, though. Before he figured out how to bankrupt an entire European country, he was a waiter and a porter on the railroads. Read: he was born poor. But he came to America, used his economics degree, and became a fully self-made billionaire.

But he also is a well-known philanthropist who uses his money to do as much good as he possibly can. He gives almost 80% of his wealth away to good causes and is passionate about promoting philanthropy. It's usually this attitude towards giving that makes him the target of politician's ire. Yet he remains one of America's billionaires and continues to follow his passion of helping people.

Takeaways from George Soros:

- Your beginnings do not dictate your endings.
- Learn how to short stocks.
- Give back to your community.

Jack Bogle

Here is another investor who rose from the ashes of the Great Depression. Jack Bogle was born in 1929 and grew up during the hardest market crash that America has ever seen. 2008 was bad, but the Great Depression was still worse. Yet he managed to make it through college and into a career in investing.

He began his career at Wellington Management, which is where he came up with the Vanguard mutual fund. Remember that name? You should, because we talked about Vanguard as one of the best mutual funds out there. He had the idea that it would be better for investors if their initial investment was spread across different funds because he knew that diversity was a key for good investments.

He really wanted to develop investments that would allow more of the average folks in the world to invest their money. This meant he worked on lowering costs for investors while also trying to raise their returns. He also focuses on trying to keep things simple, and as a result, he invests solely in United States companies. This is not a result of isolationism, but rather as a result of his unique knowledge base. Obviously, this has worked out well for him, considering he is now a billionaire.

Takeaways from Jack Bogle:

- Simple investing can be the best kind of investing.
- Lower costs can mean higher returns.
- Invest in diversity.

Ray Dalio

Add another billionaire to the list. As of summer 2018, he was worth $17.4 billion. That's an awfully nice chunk of change. He got to this point through excellent investment strategies and of course, just a little luck.

Like Warren Buffettt, Ray Dalio started his career young. He was twelve years old when he started to work as a caddie at a golf course. He worked for the type of people who tend to frequent golf-courses: investors. He overheard their conversations and took their advice. He took every dime that he made and ended up investing his earnings in Northeast Airlines. His investment ended up tripling when that airline was acquired by another. So he learned early on the value of investing in a startup company.

He continued his success and ended up forming Bridgewater Associates. This hedge fund company ended up earning well over $300 million last year. He attributes his success to one very fundamental quality: brutal honesty. He is of the opinion (and we happen to agree with him), that blatant honesty is the only way to live your life, and that includes how you invest. Because think about it, if you enter a relationship based on a lie, that relationship almost always ends in tears. And if you enter an investment based on misinformation, you could lose everything.

Takeaways from Ray Dalio:

- Be honest in everything.
- Start investing as soon as you can.
- Be patient!

Jack Welch

I wanted to add in one more inspiring character for you guys to take a look at before we end this book. Jack Welch is probably one of the most visible people in the field of economics and finance – and for good reason.

In fact, he even made a cameo on Tina Fey's breakout comedy '30 Rock.' If you haven't seen this show, I really feel sorry for you, because it is one of the best television shows of the last fifty years. Anyway, one of the main characters, Jack Donaghy, is a General Electric executive who tries to model himself after the great Jack Welch. Mr. Welch was mentioned so often in the show that he ended up doing a cameo as himself in the show. Talk about meta, right? You reach a certain level of celebrity when you get to play yourself on a television show because you are such a good businessman.

He helped make General Electric into one of the most successful countries in the world. He began there as a junior chemical engineer and worked his way up to CEO after many years of hard work and dedication. Before he became CEO of General Electric, he was the head of strategic planning for the company. This meant that he was in charge of over $2 billion dollars worth of investments for General Electric. Not only did he manage to keep that $2 billion, but he made it grow. In fact, while he was CEO, General Electric's value grew over four thousand percent. Think about that for a minute – four thousand percent. That is just an insane amount of growth for any company.

He is probably the most famous, though, for his 10% rule. Every year, he would have his junior managers rate the workers in their employ and the bottom ten percent each year would be fired. While this particular method could be considered cruel, there is no other way that he would have gotten GE's stock to grow as quickly as it did otherwise. The most interesting thing about Jack Welch, though, is that he didn't start his career in investing. He has a Ph.D in chemical engineering and a bachelor's of science in chemical engineering. Not a single one of his degrees has to do with business or investing and yet he is one, if not the most, successful businessmen of the century. And yet he was able to grow a business' value over 4000% during his tenure and also manage two billion dollars worth of assets.

So the message here is that you don't need to go back to school in order to learn how to invest well. All you really need to do is get a strong grasp on the basics and apply them well. And that is what this book is for! We want to give you the strong basics so that you can master the very basics of investing and then become an expert. Just maybe remember us when you're a billionaire.

Further Reading

Before we wrap things up for good, here is a list of the top investment books that you can look to for advice when you need it:

1. *The Little Book of Value Investing* by Tren Griffin

2. *You Can Be A Stock Market Genius: Uncover the Secret Hiding Places of Stock Market Profits* by Joel Greenblatt

3. *The Intelligent Investor: The Definitive Book on Value Investing* by Benjamin Graham

4. *The Gospel of Wealth* by Andrew Carnegie

5. *Security Analysis* by Benjamin Graham and David L. Dodd

6. *Common Stocks and Uncommon Profits* by Philip A. Fisher,

7. *Stress Test: Reflections on Financial Crises* by Tim Geithner

8. *The Essays of Warren Buffett* by Warren Buffett

9. *Jack: Straight from The Gut* by Jack Welch

10. *The Art of Value Investing: How the World's Best Investors Beat the Market* by John Heins and Whitney Tilson

11.   *The Outsiders* by William Thorndike, Jr.

12.   *The Clash of the Cultures* by John Bogle

13.   *Business Adventures: Twelve Classic Tales from the World of Wall Street* by John Brooks

14.   *Beating the Street* by Peter Lynch

15.   *Competition Demystified: A Radically Simplified Approach to Business* Strategy by Bruce Greewald

16.   *Buffettt: The Making of An American Capitalist* by Roger Lowenstein

17.   *The Little Book That Still Beats the Market* by Joel Greenblatt

18.   *A Random Walk down Wall Street: The Time-Tested Strategy for Successful Investing* by Burton Malkiel

19.   *Applied Value Investing: The Practical Application of Benjamin Graham and Warren Buffett's Valuation Principles to Acquisitions, Catastrophe Pricing* Execution by Joseph Calandro, Jr.

20.   *The Alchemy of Finance* by George Soros

These are great source of knowledge for the beginning investor. It is important to realize that the more knowledge you have about the stock market, the more successful you will be in the long run. Nobody can ever know too much about the stock market or really do too much research into the different investments that they are about to make. But it is important to know that you should not allow yourself to just get mired in investment advice and never make a move towards actually investing. Do the research, talk to the experts, and the actually make your move.

And in case you are more of a visual learner, I have also included below some of the best movies and documentaries that you can watch about the investment world:

1. Inside Job

    a. This is a documentary about the 2008 financial meltdown that happened not only in the United States but across the world. This documentary isn't just a bland regurgitation of facts about what happened; it takes place over five parts and takes the watcher inside all of the policy and history behind the crashes of 2008 and 2010. In 2010 it took home the Oscar for "best documentary."

2. The Big Short

    a. This is not a documentary, but it is very historically accurate. Plus, it has Ryan Gosling and Steve Carrell, so you know it is going to be a spectacularly acted piece of film. This is about the stock market crisis in 2008 that was precipitated by all of those bad mortgages.

    b. It follows the story of those investors who saw what was going to happen and took action to make themselves some serious money. It is an entertaining film, sort of like the Wolf of Wall Street, but it takes a more historical and serious turn. You will learn more about the financial crisis in this short film than you will if you read every news article out there on the subject.

3. Trader

    a. This takes the watcher behind the scenes of the 1987 financial crisis, just before the boom of the 1990s. In particular, it follows Paul Tudor Jones, who was a hedge fund manager who was the Nostradamus of his time. He knew that something bad was coming, but as per usual in these kinds of stories, no one listened to him. A fascinating picture.

4. 25 Million Pounds

   a. Ever want to watch a film about a financial pirate? Then this is the documentary for you. It follows the story of Nick Leeson, a real-life financial pirate who took down Barings, the bank which used to hold the Queen of England's money. It is an interesting look at those in the industry who are dishonest and the implications it has for the rest of us.

5. Frontline: Breaking the Bank

   a. Here, viewers can get a history of the policies and decisions that led to the Obama administration's famous Troubled Asset Relief Program, or TARP. It talks about how this program was used to bail out the banks, the same banks that led us into the 2008 disaster. But you know, they were too big to fail, right? Well, you can be the judge of that after you watch this insightful documentary.

6. The Ascent of Money

   a. This is the king of financial documentaries. This jewel of a film takes the viewer on a history of money and stock markets. It sounds nerdy, and it is, but it is also chock full of good information about investments and how money works. Like we keep saying, you need a good command of the basics before you can become an expert.

7. Commanding Heights: The Battle for the World Economy

   a. In a similar vein as The Ascent for Money, Commanding Heights takes the viewer through the history of globalization.

It covers events like the founding of the International Monetary Fund (IMF) and how deregulation has affected the global marketplace.

8. Life and Debt

    a. Most of us know what it's like to be in debt. And we know that it's a bad situation. This film gives you an in depth look into how debt can wreck your life. It is a valuable film to watch because even though many of us have first-hand experience with what it's like to be in debt, having an outside perspective is always useful.

9. Frontline: Inside the Meltdown

    a. This film goes inside the 2008 financial crisis, which was the largest since the Great Depression. See a pattern here? It is important to learn what we did wrong so that we don't repeat our mistakes.

10.   Frontline: Money, Power and Wall Street

    a. This film also talks about the 2008 crisis, but it's important to watch this film right after the above because it provides more context to what happened and why.

11.   The Warning

    a. This will help you see the 2008 crisis from the perspective of the people who could see it coming from a mile away
.

12.   Freakonomics: The Movie

    a. Maybe you have heard of this book – it talks about the psychology behind what drives people to invest and what makes people take what seem like insane risks. It is always interesting to take a look at what motivates people to take risks with their money.

So take some time after work, and sit in front of your television. Instead of flipping on a rerun of a show that you have seen a million times, maybe pop on something that will teach you how to make more money. We think that the book we have come up with here is a pretty great resource, but we could not possibly include every piece of advice out in the world concerning investing. We are just trying to give you a good foundation to get started. It will be a good thing for you to take the research into your own hands and find out more about the investment world.

Conclusion

Thank you so much for sticking with us throughout this book – we really do thank you. We hope that you have learned some things and are ready to get out there and invest your hard-earned cash. Let's do a quick recap of everything we covered:

1. You need to invest! Investing is the best way for you to make your money work for you. If you aren't making your money work for you, then you're effectively losing money – and nobody likes that.

2. Take advantage of handy things like compound interest, asset allocation, and diversity. Make sure that while you are definitely taking the appropriate amount of risk that you can handle so that you are maximizing your returns, you are not leaving yourself open to disaster.

3. Remember that you need to master the basics before you can become an advanced investor. Read this book, read the books that we have recommended, and watch the films that we have listed. This will give you a great foundation to build upon so that eventually you can become an expert in this field.

4. Pay attention to fees! Understand that fees can eventually erode thousands of dollars from your pocket over the years. While some of them are absolutely unavoidable, try to avoid them where you can. For example, when you are a first-time investor, remember that you don't necessarily have to find a broker and pay all of their fees. You can find a nice online platform with the minimum amount of fees and begin your foray into the marketplace that way.

5. Remember that there is more than one way to invest. You can be an active trader, where you sit in front of your computer all day long and buy and sell and trade until your fingers fall off. But this is going to require time, money, and expertise. Odds are, as a beginner investor, you are going to be short on time and

expertise. So try the other kinds of investing, like value, growth, income, and passive.

    a. Passive investments are truly great ways to make sure that you are maximizing your returns for little time actually put into the investment process. Passive investments can include things like annuities, where you just set up the fund and wait until it starts to pay you. Bonds are another great option for passive income – you just buy the bond and wait for your coupon payments.

6. There are more advanced strategies that you can use, such as short-selling, buying on the margin, and day trading. But remember, these strategies can pay off big, but they can also land you in a lot of trouble if you aren't careful. There is a reason why experts use these strategies.

7. Speaking of short selling – perhaps one of the best examples of how this pays off in the long run for some people is when people were able to see the bubble about to burst in 2008 and shorted the stock market to great financial gain. It is really one of the most fascinating tales of financial wizardry in the history of America. When millions of people lost their homes and lost their fortunes, these men walked away with billions of dollars.

8. Take a lesson from some of the greatest investors in history. Take a look at Warren Buffett, Jack Welch - see how they live their lives, spend their money, and design their investments.

9. Finally, remember that to be a good investor, you need to have the right temperament. You need to be patient – remember that good returns will take many years to realize. Stocks and bonds are not meant to be a quick investment – they are to be held for five years minimum.

So, thank you for making it through to the end of *Stock Market Investing: The Guide for Beginners*. Let's hope it was informative and able to provide you with all of the tools you need to achieve your goals. The next step is to get out there and actually invest! Use the tools we have provided you in this book and start making some money.

Finally, if you found this book useful in any way, a review on Amazon is always appreciated!

www.ingramcontent.com/pod-product-compliance
Lightning Source LLC
Chambersburg PA
CBHW051755200326
41597CB00025B/4567